Sailing Toward Faith

Bonnie-Jean Heather

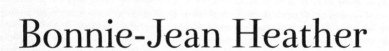

God Bless You Myrna

Bonnie

Book and Cover Design:
Vladimir Verano, Vertvolta Design

Cover photography:
Kirt Edblom ⓒⓨ 2015, via Flickr.com
Used under Creative Commons License v4.0.

References
THE HOLY BIBLE, NEW INTERNATIONAL VERSION®, NIV®
Copyright © 1973, 1978, 1984, 2011 by Biblica, Inc.™ Used by permission.

Webster (1984). *New World Dictionary of the American Language: Second College Edition.* New York, New York: Simon and Schuster.

Print ISBN: 978-0-9963437-0-1

ebook ISBN: 978-0-9963437-1-8

Dedicated to Jesus

Contents

Poems

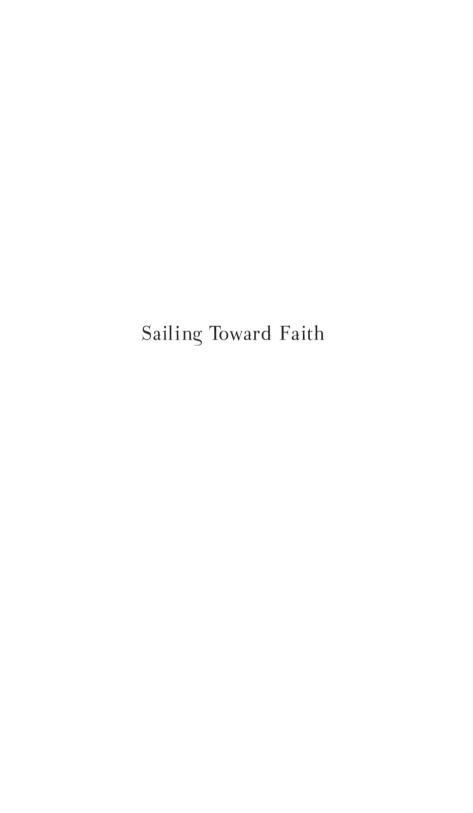

Sailing Toward Faith

Prologue

Thinking about death was her constant companion. She had to run away. She was miserable at work. Friends had abandoned her and she didn't know why. Her hurt felt fathomless and her self-worth was evaporating like the spray of a wind-swept wave. Catherine Bradley was finally grasping an understanding of what the Psalmist alluded to when he said that deep calls to deep (Psalm 42:7, New International Version). Like the Psalmist, Catherine's soul was downcast and disturbed within her (Psalm 42:5). Shame kept her from looking into the light. The dark was Catherine's covering and bitter friend.

Could she actually take her life? Catherine was afraid that by doing so she would be sent to hell for eternity. How could she know for sure that Jesus would cover even that sin? Catherine felt like her only path to sanity was to escape far away from all that she knew, all that she was clinging to as diminishing truth. Her life had become mundane and senseless. Was God also turning his back on her? She had to find out. If God was also rejecting her then she was going to die in vain anyway. Catherine needed to believe that she had a shred of worth. She needed this for her own saving grace because she had so much love she wanted to share with the world. But if the world had no use for her, then she had no use for it.

Doorstep of Heaven

I'd rather be homeless on the doorstep of heaven

Fermenting as a sin offering, becoming holy leaven

Waiting daily for manna from a merciful God

Trusting that his goodness is not mere façade

Why, on holy ground, am I perceived as useless?

The evil one is clever in his shrewdness

Smirking as my dignity is shattered

Watching me reaching, straining, for the lanyard

That would tether me safely to Christ's anchor

Bringing me home to my happily ever after

I know in eternity I'll be recognized for my worth

Sadly no one has need for my talents now on earth

Of all my sins, I know this is the worst

Please save me from this impregnable curse

And yet… "Never will I leave you; never will I forsake you" (Hebrews 13:5).

Will God grant the request of a poor sinner who cries out for help?

"Lord, help me!" she said… "Even the dogs eat the crumbs that fall from their master's table" (Matthew 15:25, 27).

Who hasn't experienced feeling like they aren't good enough? It is a lie, isn't it? Catherine was shriveling up inside and knew she had better find another way to obtain a self-esteem that would enable her to hold her head up with some semblance of dignity. She desperately needed a healing touch from the sustainer of life.

Catherine Bradley was a loner at heart and sought out solitude at every opportunity. People hurt her. So aside from her cat, her sweetest companions were often those that swim in the sea or fly high in the sky. Until such time that she found the strength she needed to be safely vulnerable, messengers of another variety prodded her toward a more understandable comprehension of truth.

When Catherine's father died, he left her his beloved sailboat along with memories of his abundant exuberance for joy. It would break his heart to know that his daughter had lost that inheritance of joy with wrong turns and foolish mistakes.

Meditative Prayer

There are times, precious Jesus, when we tend to feel like we're dead already. But in spite of this internal deception, we know that we're still alive. You promise that, "… whoever lives and believes in [you] will never die (John 11:25). Therefore, while we are still alive, take off our grave clothes and let us fully live, for you, for others, and for ourselves.

Journal Prompt

Everyone has something to live for and we must find out what that is and hold on to it for dear life. What are you holding on to? What is your one thing? Do you need to change your story?

Chapter 1

HAWK

"Why hello. We seem to have startled each other. Or have you come to give me a message?"

Was there some hidden meaning to this seemingly fortuitous encounter? Catherine Bradley was at a turning point in her life without acknowledging it in her heart. As she had done for hundreds of times, she went for an early morning walk along the shoreline. The southernmost end of Torrance Beach in Southern California was her favorite respite because of its isolation. The minute her bare feet hit the sand she felt an almost tangible peace and in unity with the surf and the seaweed that found its way onshore.

The usual pre-dawn surfers were sitting expectantly on their boards waiting for that perfect seventh wave. At that hour of the morning, except for the surfers, she almost always had the beach to herself. Gulls and terns were singing their delight at the plentiful breakfast that awaited them during the low tide. Low tide meant an easy walk on the beach because the sand at the waterline is hardened when wet. It also meant she had less of a chance of stepping on the occasional patch of tar which got washed up on the dry sand. As each wave rolled gently back into the sea, little bubbles of tiny creatures made soft popping noises as they buried themselves deeper to escape being eaten by the birds. The air was soft and gentle that morning and the ocean was restful as Catherine strolled along breathing in the salty air. The sea water felt unusually tepid as waves of white foam gently caressed her bare legs in their restless and hypnotic motion of seeking the shore, then returning to the ocean's depths. Were the waves bored, or merely confused like she felt? Back and forth they played upon her senses. The beseeching sand was enticing her with each step until she plopped down rather ungracefully and followed her busily drifting thoughts until they were quieted and her emotions were still inside. Finally she was at one with nature and blessed by all that she saw sprawling out before her. The bay is quite large. The low-lying hills of Santa Monica in the distance to the north, and the gentle sloping cliffs of Palos Verdes just to her left were hazy in the light fog that was rapidly dissipating as the sun overpowered the morning.

Catherine loved the beach with an insatiability that never seemed to go away, yet she knew it was time to move on. Her restless soul and aching heart were itching to go north. She had no idea where she wanted to go specifically. All she knew was that she had to escape the tedium of a thankless job and the encroaching danger that lurked at every turn in the big city of Los Angeles, and inside of her.

Walking back along the beach she was filled with a sadness mixed with a growing elation about what the future might hold for her. As Catherine was nearing the path at the end of the beach that would take her up the hill and back to her car, there it was. The hawk startled Catherine and held her captive in awe as it blocked her passage. Its wings were keeping it in the air, but it wasn't moving from its location, and it was looking right at her. Questioningly, she stared back at this amazing creature. Like an angelic being it seemed to be telling her something and she strained to decipher its message. She was struck motionless as they communicated in silence for a few moments. Then it flew away. Had she only imagined it? What do angels look like anyway?

Catherine couldn't explain it logically, but birds were her burning bush. When she saw three birds flying together in a sky otherwise bereft of any other birds, she felt like she was receiving a word from God. It was his acknowledgement to Catherine that he saw her. Moses had an inextinguishable fire to get his attention. Catherine had birds to ignite her passion toward the love she hungered for in Jesus. The hawk was her first messenger; or at least the first one she recognized. She was taught about Jesus as a child, so she knew about him. But she didn't really know him. She thanks her parents for giving her this foundation of curiosity toward faith.

Meditative Prayer

In the darkness, you are seen

In the emptiness, your presence is felt

In shallow prayers, you hear us

In the bitterness of life, your sweetness can be tasted

And we will call you, Immanuel

Journal Prompt

After being in the desert for a long time, Moses was most likely insatiably hungry to meet with God. He, too, had an inextinguishable fire. How can we keep our fire alive? How can we live so that others see our tongues of fire?

Chapter 2

FOG

Sophia, her feline friend, and Catherine, in a William Garden-designed Gulf 32-foot sloop-rigged sailboat named Whispering Spirit, departed Redondo Beach for yet another adventure crossing the channel for a weekend excursion to Catalina Island. Catherine called it an adventure because it seemed she always had some new lesson to learn about sailing every time she left the slip. Sophia stayed below deck and curled up in her favorite spot on the V-berth to cat nap while the sea rocked her to sleep. Catherine honestly did not know what she would do without her. Sophia offered a solace that people couldn't, or wouldn't.

It was a picture-perfect sail. The sun was glistening and the wind was blowing at a steady pace off the starboard side of the boat and a little to the stern allowing Whispering Spirit to make headway at its hull speed of 15 knots (17.3 miles per hour). Sitting in the cockpit with her left foot steering the wheel, while feeling the sun on her face and the wind blowing through her hair, was Catherine's idea of experiencing a touch from heaven. It was warm enough to wear shorts and a sleeveless t-shirt. It would be smart to wear tennis shoes, but she always preferred to go barefoot on sunny days. Catherine normally kept her shoulder-length hair in a ponytail to keep the wind from blowing it in her face. But that day it just felt wonderful to let it flow freely. She would tie it up once she got to the island. Spending so much time in the sun added sun streaks to Catherine's already blonde hair. Not even the slight correction needed to avoid

The Purr of Reason

I'm becoming ever invisible to all but my cat

I whisper to her what's screaming within

She purrs all knowing

As the center of my attention, her world is complete

collision with a tanker crossing the shipping lanes disturbed her sense of harmony with such a perfect day.

The ocean has a personality all its own. It has mood changes just like we do. Today the water seems happy and the gentle wavelets are frolicking like ballerinas as they plié softly up and down slapping against the hull in a hypnotic rhythm. Catherine was nearly blinded as she watched the sun's effects brilliantly touching the tips of each tiny blue wave. Steadily Whispering Spirit made headway. Her sails were full. Catherine could picture Mr. Wind blowing gently into Whispering Spirit's billowing jib and mainsail. The water was making lapping noises against the hull as Catherine breathed in the sublime saltiness of a vast ocean. Catalina beckoned as a misty barren brown whose features remained unclear for a while longer. For this moment Catherine was in control. There was no danger lurking. All was well in her world. She lifted her face to the sun, closed her eyes, and felt the motion of Whispering Spirit's progress. Catherine was alone and yet she felt the presence of God, the birds in the air, and the fullness of a world unseen right below the keel. What a lovely sail! No one could hurt her out on the deep blue ocean.

Oil tankers were Catherine's nemesis. You can't compete with them. You can only steer clear of their largeness and momentum. Although sailboats normally do have the right of way over power boats, any dummy could see the fallacy of insisting on having the right of way with an oil tanker that often reaches over 1,000 feet in length. Catherine heard a story often told amongst yachties about a tanker entering the port of San Pedro with a sailboat mast stuck to its bow. That's a chilling enough story to make any sailor wary. It seemed Catherine almost never sailed the channel without having to give way to at least one of these monsters crossing her path. The trick was to make sure you were pointing into the wave of their trailing wake. Catherine learned that lesson once when she got sloppy and didn't point Whispering Spirit into the oncoming wave of a tanker's wake. All hell broke loose below decks. Books went flying. Sophia went flying. Everything that was on the table went flying. What a mess! It was a good lesson though. Catherine hung some bungee cords across the bookshelf and learned to stow everything away while sailing. Sophia always took refuge after that in the V-berth. She never quite trusted Catherine again to brave the salon for safety while under way. Another outcome of that adventure was to devise straps that went the length of the port-side settee across from the dinette to hold her securely while napping. Although she never adjusted to sleeping below decks while underway, she could grab some quick naps while far enough off shore to feel somewhat safe. Oftentimes there were even some anchorages that were rough enough for Catherine to choose the divan instead of the V-berth to keep her snug.

Catalina Island loomed ever nearer with the details of Emerald Cove getting more distinct by the minute. It was an aptly named harbor. The water, a luminous green, sparkled like emeralds in the late afternoon sun. Catherine was in luck. She called the Harbor Master on the VHF radio and they assigned her a spot which was wonderfully close to shore in the second row of mooring wands. She liked being this close to land so she could do some snorkeling around the rocks without having to swim a long distance from the boat. Not too many boats had arrived as yet and she had plenty of space to maneuver comfortably in the anchorage to scoop up the mooring wand and settle Whispering Spirit in for a peaceful evening.

There's quite an art to picking up a mooring wand. Mooring wands are all those sticks you can see from shore floating throughout the various anchorages off Catalina Island. You have to approach the wand very slowly with the engine in neutral; that is, unless you are experienced enough to approach under sail alone which Catherine wasn't. You have to be close enough to reach over the bow railings to grab the wand. Then you grab the spreader line attached to the wand, get it under the bow pulpit and tie it to the bow cleat. You then walk the spreader line aft and tie it to the stern cleat as quickly as possible after cinching up the slack. Laying the mooring wand on the deck instead of simply letting it float in the water will keep it from clanking against the hull. It helps to have a boat mooring hook handy just in case you don't get close enough to grab the wand. Out of curiosity Catherine jumped over the side into the water, took a deep breath, and followed the line down through clear water. It was attached to a cement block which was big enough and heavy enough to keep a boat secure in the severest of storms. The wands are sectioned off with the smaller boats close to shore and the larger ones further off.

The yachties arriving all seemed to be in a great mood. Soon the dinghies were out in force with people visiting friends who had come over together to enjoy the weekend. Buddy boating was the fad. I guess people felt safer if they knew friends were alongside. Maybe it's like women who can't seem to powder their noses all by themselves. But most boating captains are men and you never see them traipsing off to the men's room together. How weird that they felt the need to keep their buddies nearby at sea. In the anchorage there were inflatable soft dinghies, hard dinghies, and even eight-foot Sabots – the smallest of sailboats, all maneuvering about having fun. The noise was deafening with the screams of happy children, outboard motors, and generators running to ensure there would be enough ice for drinks during cocktail hour. It was fun watching all the excitement. It was time to enjoy a quick swim in the cool refreshing water before preparing a simple dinner of steaming clam chowder soup poured into a fresh sourdough bread bowl with some raspberries swimming in half-n-half cream for dessert.

As night began to darken the evening skies, the noise slowly dissipated and people headed below decks to enjoy some rest after their busy day. Being tied to a mooring wand meant having a peaceful evening of sleep. Personally Catherine thought this was even more secure than being anchored. When Whispering Spirit was anchored, she always felt the need to keep checking whether or not the anchor was still holding. But that night she enjoyed a sound sleep. It was warm enough to leave the V-berth hatch open and the gentle night air wafted down through the opening to caress her face. Being surrounded by other boaters offered safety with no need to lock the cabin doors. How sad that this freedom was diminishing for land lubbers. Boaters look out for one another. There's a sense of danger when you are floating on the water that tends to develop camaraderie amongst the boaters for safety. It's like being a member of a church knowing you have responsibility to care for one another.

Sometime during the early morning hours a chill had set in

and Catherine groggily awoke just to close the hatch before falling quickly back to sleep. In the morning she found Whispering Spirit enveloped in fog. It was the densest fog she had ever experienced. From the cockpit she couldn't even see the bow of the boat. The chill created a feeling of coziness and she lazily hunkered below with a hot cup of coffee and a good book while waiting for the sun to do its magic and restore clarity.

But there was something nagging at her. The closed-in sensation of the fog made her feel like she was in a womb of sorts. Her thoughts were being sucked inward as she withdrew into an emptiness that was hard to define. It was a time for reflection and all kinds of thoughts about life and what it means to be alive. Why did she keep seeking solitude? Why was she forever trying to escape from humanity? If she was running away from something; then, in balance, was there something she was trying to run toward?

Like Saint Augustine Catherine sensed a need to pick up and read the Bible that was kept on the bookshelf over the divan. She didn't know why she felt the need to do this because she hadn't touched the book in eons. It was just another type of anchor that was a necessity for any decent book collection. Catherine felt drawn to the Book of Samuel because she vaguely remembered something special about God calling out to Samuel. Maybe he had some words of wisdom for her too. Then, without so much as a warning, tears started rolling down her face while she read. She felt like she could cry without embarrassment because no one could hear her in the fog with all sounds muted because of the density of the air. Catherine was alone in her mysterious misery. Then she heard something. Jesus? No – it couldn't possibly be God. Could it? Jesus? God kept calling Samuel and Samuel thought it was Eli calling his name. Eli was the priest whose custody Samuel was placed under. But it was not Eli. It was God. Eli realized what was happening and told Samuel how to respond the next time he heard his name called. When Samuel responded as directed, God gave him a message. God has different messages for each of his children. His message for Catherine was different from his message to Samuel. We all have different callings because we are all uniquely created for a purpose.

Unlike Samuel, she did know God when he called her, but she hadn't dusted him off of her cobwebbed heart for many years. Now he had her full attention. Tears of remorse kept falling down Catherine's cheeks as she cried in sorrow over shelving the Lord she had once felt so close to in her youth. The fog was his gift to her. She felt like a child being held in the safety of his protective embrace.

She spent the rest of the day just trying to understand. And yet trying to make sense of it all was futile. She knew what she had to do. Catherine had to find her way back to God. In selfish pursuit, she wanted to continue on in her solidarity until she could find some answers to a perplexity she could not even define. But now there was purpose. Catherine knew what she had to do. It was time to seriously pursue the dream of heading out to sea and finding her destiny in the arms of the love of her savior. She was entering into, consciously and decisively, a quest that would take her on a journey into unknown waters of both a physical and spiritual depth.

Catherine had a lot of questions. How does she learn to get acquainted with her spirit, this shadowy mystery that she knows is a part of her, a part of her that she longed to know, yet remained a stranger? How does she find the truth of who she really is? How does she honor the core of who God made her to be? If she abuses the outer shell of her deeper self, then how does she begin to heal that part of her that she can't see or touch? Catherine knew, without being able to explain how, that there was a fuller her that was more than mere breath and blood. She had a feeling that her thoughts held somewhat of a clue as to the mystery of who she really was. She hoped her sojourn would begin to clear away some of the fog that hid her inner truth, and that God would speak to her clearly, or yell if need be. She knew she would recognize his voice whether he whispered or felt the need to blast his fog horn to get her attention.

When Catherine was safely anchored, there was no need for the horn that she kept stowed in the quarter berth. Yet when she was underway, especially at night when it was dark and the fog lay heavy around Whispering Spirit, the fog horn helped her to be heard, and therefore seen, by other boaters. Low visibility created a lot of tension in her shoulders as she gripped the wheel straining to see through the

TARGET

By his stripes we are healed

By his grace we are revealed

How deeply we have missed the mark

Now turned around and ready to embark

on a journey where our faces seek his light

Darkness rules no longer as we hunger for his sight

to watch over us each new day

as we live and work and pray

to Messiah God of healings

who deeply cares about our feelings

dense pea soup. Her hearing became more astute as well. She was tuned in to the rhythm of the swells. If they all of a sudden changed direction, it was possible a ship was out in front of her. She had radar, and that was helpful, but there's so much more comfort in actually being able to see your surroundings. She likes the image of a horn as strength. The Bible has many references to a horn and its magical powers. Psalm 18:2 says, "The LORD is my rock, my fortress and my deliverer; my God is my rock, in whom I take refuge, my shield and the horn of my salvation, my stronghold." Catherine liked to think of a horn when her thoughts or her surroundings were fuzzy and unclear. Listening with all her senses gave her added clarity.

Holy Spirit whispered a caution to Catherine. She had been on a different kind of collision course with the pull to new-age spirituality. She realized that God was steadfastly steering her vessel into deeper waters of faith to keep her from running aground in the murky shallows of empty meditative practices. How can anyone know him if they are trying to empty their mind? That made no sense. The way to find God is to give all one's attention to him, not focus on not focusing on him. That was just plain weird! And it wasn't working for her anyway, so giving up that practice was a relief.

Heading back that evening to Redondo Beach under a full moon and the slip in Portofino Marina meant a lot of powering in dismally overcast weather. But Catherine's heart was light enough to soar with the seagulls flying overhead seeking their own tidbits of sustenance. Her head was clear and ready for answers, and full of love, something she hadn't felt in a very long time.

All was in order for Catherine to drift away for a very different kind of season of her life as she sought to find her worth in God. She gathered up her courage and did everything that was necessary to leave for ports unknown sometime the following month. The first thing she did was move onboard. Her apartment lease was ready to expire anyway. It was God's perfect timing. One of her brothers was ready to live alone and moved into what they lovingly referred to as the *wee hoos* with all her furniture. Catherine absolutely loved living aboard Whispering Spirit in the marina. It was a bit of a challenge working in the real world and living on a sailboat, especially getting ready in the morning, but she didn't mind. She drastically downsized her working wardrobe to just a few outfits that she could mix and match for the month she had left. Leaving her company at that time worked out well because her boss was retiring. He had been getting progressively grouchy the past couple of years making life miserable as he impatiently waited for his last day to arrive so he could spend his days golfing. Happily we were both off to new adventures and experienced no parting sadness.

Catherine had to shower up at the marina office which really wasn't a problem like it might have been for others. She took pride in being able to rough it which was probably a throw back from her camping and back-packing days. The hardest part for her was selling her powder blue, perfectly running, unmarred super beetle. She loved that car.

In addition to mechanical how-to-books, and her dusted-off Bible, her bookshelves were now graced with books written by Christian authors, along with several varieties of classic literature. Paperwork was in order. The engine was checked and re-checked. The rigging was checked as well. She bought as many charts as she could find on Baja and Central America.

Whispering Spirit had been hauled and dry docked for a few days while she put a fresh coat of anti-fouling bottom paint on the keel. Then she oiled all the exterior teak, a project she really enjoyed, especially while working on a warm sunny day. Catherine felt like an artist and undoubtedly took longer than was necessary to complete the task. It felt terribly wrong having her beautiful boat sitting unnaturally on land, and even stranger having to climb a ladder to board her from a cemented parking lot in a ship yard. She couldn't wait to get Whispering Spirit back in the water where she belonged. And then it felt so absurd watching Whispering Spirit being towed down Pacific Coast Highway as if she were sailing on land. Catherine drove behind her fretting like a protective lion with her only cub. Before gently setting Whispering Spirit back into her natural habitat, Catherine spanked her beautifully refurbished bottom with a bottle of champagne.

Empty spaces under the seats in the main salon, in the quarter berth, and in the storage compartment under the forward berth were well stocked with canned goods and other non-perishables. Some friends gave her a large bagful of avocados from their yard as a parting gift. It would be quite the challenge figuring out how to be creative eating all those delicious avocados that would ripen at the same time so as to not reach the point where she never wanted to see another avocado for the rest of her life. She kept all her fresh produce in a netted bag that swung from a hook in the bulkhead to keep them from getting bruised while underway.

Sailing south was a quest that Catherine had to fulfill before heading north to God's country. She had never been to the Pacific Northwest and didn't know anyone from that area, but there was just something about living in a land full of trees and lakes and snow-capped mountains that tugged at her heart strings. She envisioned big open spaces and wanted so much to live with space around her.

Although Catherine thought anyone who declared they were going to conquer the sea was a fool, she felt qualified to venture out on her own based on years of sailing in Southern California to places like Catalina Island, the Channel Islands, and Santa Barbara Island. The sea cannot be conquered. That is like boasting that one is going to conquer God – it can't be done. One can only use their best skills at sea, and one can only bow before the Creator of the sea. A couple of times she bare-boat chartered a sailboat with a couple of friends in the Virgin Islands. Bare-boating simply meant renting a boat without a captain. The Caribbean is captivatingly beautiful. When she kept the boat on a path sailing between St. Thomas, St. John, Jost Van Dyke, Tortola, and Virgin Gorda, they experienced smooth sailing. But when she ventured outside Sir Frances Drake Channel for a brief excursion, they encountered ferocious winds. She was reminded of the boundaries God has for us. Catherine felt safe when she stayed within the confines he established for those who follow him. When she ventured outside of his boundaries and into the deep waters of sin, her calm was disturbed by the storm within her. Catherine came to understand what the Psalmist declared when he referred to God's rod and staff bringing comfort (Psalm 23:4).

Reflecting back, Catherine first began learning about sailing when her father took her and her brothers out when they were all young. She also took lessons in an eight-foot Sabot, a fourteen-foot Capri, and a thirty-three foot Erickson. She took navigation classes at the local community college and also with the Power Squadron. She embarrassingly had to admit that trying to navigate the stars with a sextant was a skill she never really mastered. Her first practice lesson trying to locate the stars through a sextant was while standing on the beach where she promptly fell over backwards. The Power Squadron offered Basic Boating, Seamanship, Piloting, and Navigation classes which Catherine felt should be a requirement for all sailors. It still stuns her that we need a driver's license for the road, but not a license to be out on the water. She also studied and got her Amateur Radio General Class license so she could operate the ham radio while at sea. She took some first aid classes and assembled a serious medical kit with the help of one of her brothers who was a medic. She also had an extensive tool kit with spare parts for most of the mechanical workings of the boat, not that she was experienced with many of the mechanical operations, but she figured she could always ask for help.

Whispering Spirit is such a beautiful sailboat. Catherine is tall, which made the pilot house a dream for her since she could stand upright in the galley and look out the large forward-facing windows while cooking. It had a full keel that added stability and a sense of security for extended off-shore sailing. The Perkins diesel engine was almost always reliable. There was a haus pipe that fed the anchor chain down into the locker of the bow by simply stepping on a motorized button on the foredeck. This made the whole anchoring process so much easier than having to physically hand haul an anchor onboard, especially when single handling. Having a rigid dinghy on davits off the stern could be a little tricky to maneuver, but it was manageable. There was also an eight foot inflatable soft dinghy that was kept tied down on the foredeck and very easy to launch. All she had to do was toss it over the life lines while hanging on to the painter. The self-furling jib made her feel positively spoiled. She no longer had to haul various sail bags to the foredeck, hook the sail to the forestay, and thread lines back to the cockpit. It was not only a lot of work to have multiple jibs, but it could also be quite hazardous to hoist sails on the foredeck in inclement weather.

The salon below decks was beautifully decorated with lots of storage. The settee had a lovely fabric that was a gold-colored patchwork design. The starboard dining area had a table that could be lowered and made into an additional sleeping berth whenever friends came along. The table was also a great place to spread out charts which were kept stored in the quarter berth aft of the galley. The quarter berth was designed for sleeping, but proved very useful for storage and could easily turn into a junk closet if not careful. The sloping sides of the V-berth were carpeted making it comfy to sit against and acted like another room. The gimbaled stove was essential for cooking on a rocking boat. The galley sink faced forward making it almost a delight to do dishes since she could look out the large windows. There were separate foot pumps for both a fresh-water and a salt-water spigot. Most of the dishwashing at sea was done with salt water; laundry too for that matter. It was only while in a crowded anchorage that she succumbed to washing with fresh water because of the sewage from all the boats. You have to get over a lot of unpleasantries when cruising.

Meditative Prayer

Lord, make our entwining links of confusion anchored to your solid mysterious core. Please be the rock solid still point embedded in our warring members where we can return time and time again. The battle is wearying. We need you to shelter us so that we may surface with courage to breathe deeply of your Spirit.

Journal Prompt

As we sail through our busy lives, how can we learn to savor the moment? What if the quiet moment was that which we protect to reflect upon in times of stress? The moment is the time in between activities. It is our precious link to Jesus. The moment is important to God. He wants to know he's being thought of just like we want to know that God is thinking about us. Let's make the moment the most important time of our day.

Chapter 3

THE QUEST BEGINS

Catherine wondered if she was being obedient and following God's directive for her to leave her country and her family and go to the land he would show her just like he directed Abraham's footsteps. Was she following and trusting God even before she had fully acknowledged his presence in her heart? Don't atheists choose to believe in the goodness of the universe without being able to explain why they believe this? Catherine believed the cup of life was more on the full side with evil falling somewhere below the midline. God was the only author she knew who encouraged his readers to sneak a peek at the last chapter so they don't have to fear the scary parts leading up to the end of the historical drama as it unfolds. She could hardly wait for the sequel of where God will take her when his Kingdom on earth begins anew.

There were no well-wishers on the docks to see her and her furry friend off that fateful day in the early autumn of 1980 as they headed off to the great unknown for whatever adventures God had in store for them. Catherine named her cat Sophia in the hope that she would be her wisdom, and she was going to need a lot of wisdom on this cruising adventure. She found a particularly beautiful Scripture verse that refers to wisdom: "But whoever listens to me will live in safety and be at ease, without fear of harm" (Proverbs 1:33). Adventures can be dangerous undertakings and Catherine didn't want fear to get in the way of what she felt called to do. Sophia proved herself to be a wonderful first mate. She helped Catherine not to feel so alone. God bless pets!

She spent a lot of time training her feline friend to use the potty on board. It really wasn't all that difficult. She used a plastic bowl that fit just inside the rim of the toilet bowl and filled it with litter. Then she removed the lid (man's dream come true). Gradually the litter in the bowl was removed. The last step required having no litter at all with a hole in the bottom of the plastic bowl until eventually the plastic bowl was removed altogether. The head door had an open space at the bottom so Sophia could come and go as she pleased. This worked out really well for Catherine – no kitty litter to mess with. The only problem arose when they both had to use the potty at the same time. You wouldn't think cats had the ability to give dirty looks, but she could when interrupted.

The wind had been blowing steadily all week before the scheduled departure date and it added to the excitement to get underway. Careless sailboat owners who don't tie the mainsail halyard off to a spreader or lifeline cause a cacophony of noise as the lines clank against the mast on a windy day. Although a nuisance to most boat owners, secretly Catherine loved the sound. It made the boats seem alive, like they were demanding their freedom from the slip where they remained dormant for most of their life. Sailboats are meant for the wind – not cocktail happy hours as their only excuse for existence.

The air was refreshingly cool with a gentle breeze blowing that pre-dawn of Catherine's departure. The world was asleep when she awoke and made final preparations making sure everything loose was stowed away properly. With the engine in neutral, Catherine walked Whispering Spirit out of her slip while holding on to the lifeline stanchion. As she turned Whispering Spirit's nose toward the marina's channel, Catherine hopped onboard and put the engine in gear. The other sailboats seemed to mourn their lack of freedom as they cheered encouragement with their rigging gently clapping against their masts.

The rock jetty in the main part of the channel kept the water calm as Catherine went forward to raise the main. The only visitors there to see her off were squawking seagulls. She thought they were cheering her bravado. Actually, they were screeching out a warning as Catherine proceeded to run into the mid-channel buoy. So much for being an experienced sailor! She hadn't even made it out of the marina without making a complete fool of herself. Those feathered friends' squawking ended up sounding more like belly laughs. FINE!

The waves came at Catherine as she rounded the jetty and departed the marina for the last time. The early morning sky was dimly lit with the city lights of Palos Verdes playing peek-a-boo in the light fog off the port side. It wasn't long before the cliffs of Palos Verdes ended and she was in the shipping lane powering for a short distance before unfurling the jib. Although the wind was mild, Catherine knew it had enough strength to keep Whispering Spirit making some forward progress, at least for as long as her patience lasted. Finally she couldn't stand the noise a minute longer. It was time for the music to start so she cut the engine and there it was – instant bliss – silence (which was music to Catherine's ears). The masthead light was her contribution to the hazy morning. She was truly alone out on the ocean except for the oil tanker that would inevitably cross her path. The magic continued as she listened to Whispering Spirit gently moving through the water. This was peace. This was internal stillness in motion. This is God. A gull flew silently overhead. She was watched over from above.

It was good to get away to live in isolation with her God. Catherine needed to allow time and space to begin her healing process. She needed to somehow shed her outer garment of skin that she had allowed to be abused for so long. She needed to allow God to scrape off the dirt so that she could begin to see a holier creation Jesus intended that she experience. Catherine wanted the warmth of Mexico's waters and sunshine to embrace her like Jesus does and slough off life's absurdities of needless shame. What if she were to cherish her body in the way that God intended? Touch, whether physical, emotional, or spiritual, would from now on be sacred. Sacred physical touch is the kind that is blessed within the confines of marriage. It can also be experienced when holding a child, or comforting a friend in their sorrow. Sacred touch also means being able to receive genuine kindness from another. Why is it so hard, Catherine wondered, for her to receive? Undoubtedly it was because of the need for protective control that she perceived she had over situations – and pride – yes, definitely pride. Pride is a tough barrier to pierce. It is like a last remaining fortress. If no one could touch her, then no one could hurt her. Who wins in this game? Who loses?

Does God sometimes take our strength away in order to entice us to return to him? It seemed to Catherine that some people take hold of God's almightiness so much better than she was able to do. The strength of others faith seemed greater than hers. While at sea, she hoped to be able to graduate with a higher degree than the ones she'd received at the university. She wanted to learn well in the midst of her muddled confusion before it was time to return to a land-based home – wherever that might turn out to be. She wanted to know without any doubts whatsoever that God exists and cares about her. She had much to learn about faith. The timing seemed right. She was in her middle thirties and burned out from working really long hours in personnel management when her boss announced his retirement. She knew that if she was going to do this cruising thing, she'd better do it while she was still young enough and strong enough to single hand Whispering Spirit. Two years at sea was the maximum time Catherine had allotted before going back to the real world. Her graduate program had a lot to do with learning about poverty in different cultures. Cruising south of the border would be twofold. She would be learning firsthand about other cultures in the developing world; and she was going to be witnessing the financial poverty of others in the midst of her own spiritual impoverishment. Poverty takes on many forms. Catherine wanted to learn what it meant to live under grace. She sensed others would be able to teach her about grace while living one day at a time with the God who loves all his children, no matter the culture or circumstances.

Catherine's first destination was familiar Avalon Cove on Catalina Island. Leaving early usually meant a low ceiling and a sluggish crawl until the wind picked up. But that was the price she was always willing to pay for getting underway before sunrise. The wind typically didn't start blowing steadily until the fog lifted some time mid-morning or early afternoon. She just happened to be in luck with at least a gentle wind blowing this day. For some reason, she was always in a hurry to get to her destination. Being an early bird normally exacerbated the problem of sailing without ideal wind and weather conditions. And getting underway when there was fog meant having to crank up the Iron Jenny in order to make any progress, or suffer just slugging along at a snail's pace. An Iron Jenny is a term that describes the engine. Jenny refers to the Genoa sail that is larger than a jib, which means you can go faster in a good wind. Good old George often did most of the steering in long passages. Whoever created the auto pilot was a genius. Catherine had grown to trust this mechanical wonder that she nick-named George. That morning as the wind remained light, she had about four hours of either allowing her mind to go numb and just vacantly stare at an un-taut mainsail and jib annoyingly flapping ad nauseum in a bare whisper of wind, or she could do something useful with her time and rejuvenate her mind. So rather than allow herself to come dangerously close to nodding off, she decided to write.

Catherine found a beautifully bound leather journal while shopping for non-essentials to entertain her on the journey. She didn't really know what sparked the idea for this title, but it absolutely encapsulates the theme of her enfolding story.

⌒ *Sailing Toward Faith* ⌒

God is Catherine's Captain. He was guiding her vessel of doubts and confusion. Her self-appointed quest was to discover deeply and once and for all if there truly was a God; and, if so, to find out if she could be unconditionally loved. And if she was unconditionally loved, did that make her worthy? And if she was worthy, what exactly was it that made her worthy? So often she found herself drawn to the pleading of a loving father who said to Jesus "I do believe; help me overcome my unbelief!" (Mark 9:24). Catherine believed, but her faith was weak and still in the mustard-seed stage of her quest. She longed for it to blossom and have all doubts removed. From the bottom of her heart she prayed… Please help me my Captain to find you.

Catherine thought herself to be an adventuress of the high seas. But at the same time she was a vulnerable child seeking the affirmation of her Heavenly Father approaching God humbly in her false bravado. Such a dichotomy was difficult to unfold. Are we to be brave? Or are we to be humble? Can we be both? Respect had been a constant absence in her life and Catherine desperately longed for this elusive treasure. Surely God is a respecter of women. There are so many Bible stories that confirm this line of reasoning. She just needed to find a way to own it for herself. Once she began trusting that God could respect her, she knew she could open the door to trusting that others could respect her as well.

Catherine had finally reached a stage in her life where she had outgrown, hopefully anyway, the pathetic stages of a youthful stubbornness to keep making dumb choices. Could the God of the universe look down upon her with respect? After failed marriages, she wasn't feeling much like someone who deserved respect. But Holy Spirit prompts us toward rebirth and renewal. And if we can be reborn, then surely we can become the person God wants us to be, right? Catherine wanted God to see her as a confident woman who could hold her head up high without shame. Now she just wanted to live with dignity. She imagined God seeing her as his child yet also as a fully-grown woman who was capable, loving, and filled with integrity. Was she just dreaming that God could see through her mistakes to a different her that was desirous of turning her life around and beginning all over again?

All of us experience pain and it is not something to be ignored or downplayed. Yet Catherine felt guilty when she made an attempt to honor the pain she had known in her life. She felt ashamed for comparing her story with that of so many others whose lives were horrifically embellished in unimaginable pain. But pain and suffering were real to her without comparing it to what others experience.

Catherine knew that part of the healing process involved forgiving those who hurt us. What does it look like to forgive others? How do we forgive? Does forgiving require contact with the one who hurt us? Could forgiveness simply be an inward heart kind of thing? What if the person is no longer in our life? Should we find them and tell them we've forgiven them and ask for their forgiveness? What if that only opens closed wounds? Is it right to open up wounds that have been scabbed over? If we do reach out to forgive and ask forgiveness, are we only salving our own conscience? Is it kind to re-open wounds? Maybe this is a matter to confer personally with God about. Maybe each situation is different. Maybe it is kinder sometimes to just do the inward work. As mere mortals, Catherine believed pain lingers but that it can also be softened over time, making us more pliable and useful to others.

It was impossible for Catherine to understand how anyone would say no to Jesus when he beckons us to follow him. While at sea, she was confident she would find him, and by finding him she would discover her true destiny. She wanted the numbness of that first kindling spark to grow ablaze again and tingle her back to life.

When Catherine was younger, Satan fooled her into thinking that she was stupid. Young women can be so hard on themselves. We allow the lies to creep into our thinking. In our desperate attempts to compete with the images of external beauty affronting our senses on a daily basis, we seek approval from others instead of Jesus. The mirror seems cruel as we fight with it to conjure up the image we want to see in the looking glass. In spite of false images, why can't we simply see ourselves as God sees us? There is no one more important to want to please anyway.

If Catherine had the power to change one thing in this world, she would have all her sisters in Christ see themselves as Jesus sees them, even as he sees her. She heard someone once say that *God don't make junk.* Imagine a world where the looking glass only reflected the image that Jesus sees when he looks at us. As she held up her face to receive his love, she offered praise to her creator, "…because I am fearfully and wonderfully made" (Psalm 139:14). If God is happy with what he sees through the work of his only Son, then who are we to argue? Such love as this is too wonderful. Catherine knew she must find a way to believe it.

DESTINY

Talitha Koum, little girl, get up

Don't let your sorrows keep you down

You've too much to offer to let burdens interrupt

The work you've yet to do before receiving your crown

He created you in wonder as a very special girl

The grittiness of life transformed now into pearl

Let your luster be a reflection of the love you have for Him

Shining out in all directions singing with His Seraphim

Pay attention to those plans He's destined just for you

Take pleasure in His Glory as He daily makes you new

Catherine tried over and over again throughout her life to prove that she was worthy. Fighting this kind of battle was supremely exhausting. She could never win this war alone. Only God could lift her out of this ash heap of striving. Father God – Jesus – Holy Spirit – One God in Three Persons –who is clearly before her yet is somehow riddled in mystery all the while filling her with hope.

Speaking of himself, Jesus told Paul that he is "a servant by the commission God gave (him) to present to you the word of God in its fullness – the mystery that has been kept hidden for ages and generations, but is now disclosed to the Lord's people" (Colossians 1:25-26). Catherine's faith in the middle of her life's crisis was the only way to restoring her ashes to life. Catherine died to him. But that was a far cry from being dead to him. She felt and embraced the light within her soul that cried lonely but not alone. Yet each step upward seemed only to cause her to fall a rung lower. She couldn't do this anymore. She couldn't keep fighting to prove her worthiness. She wanted to die. She wanted to live. Each gain in accomplishment meant the loss of another beat in a heart and body that was limited. But her soul knows the way. She must trust in the knowing unknowable Christ. Death is too easy. If Jesus was dead within her, she could simply let the unthinkable happen. But in her sleep, she sees his light. The tiniest flicker is brighter than a volcano of flowing desire. For now she can rest and let the waves of fear wash over her. When she thinks she's reached the bottom of despair, she knows her feet will discover a solid foundation and find the strength to push mightily until she breaks through to the light. And there she will have her answer. God will not allow her striving to be for naught.

Forgive a brief interlude down memory lane. Why is it that all the things she accomplished never left her satisfied that she was good enough? And why on earth do we feel the need to compete with others? God made each of us unique and fashioned us in love. Why can't we find wholeness in just being who we are? Catherine felt barren inside, bereft of proper thinking about the woman she had hoped others would see. She wondered how many women, like her, were striving to try and justify worth through acts of achievement. Isn't the applause of Jesus enough?

Another one of her strivings was learning how to ski. She discovered that she had a serious competitive spirit. She wondered if she was competitive to prove something to others, or to herself. She wondered what God thought about competition? Paul made a comment about completing a race. By learning to ski, was she seeking some kind of reward? Rather than her efforts being selfish, maybe the reward was simply that of gaining confidence. And, as a more confident woman, she felt she could be a blessing to others. Why must everything be such an internal struggle? Why can't we just *be* at times without trying to defend everything?

For several years Catherine left work on a Friday afternoon with friends headed for Mammoth and drove the six long hours for a weekend of skiing. Though tedious, the drive always instilled in her the deepest sense of awe. After bumper-to-bumper traffic followed by the drive through Mojave Desert, they would finally enter the sweetest part of the trip. Little town followed by sweet little town displayed majestic mountains arising just outside the car's windows. Crystal clear skies shimmering with stars unseen while in the city now lit up the sky outside of the warmth and rhythm of the car's motion. Listening to gentle piano music filled the senses with heaven's purest aura. For the first couple of years, she could not get out of a chair lift without falling flat on her face. Thankfully that embarrassing time passed. Then Catherine had a run that she could feel proud about. It wasn't a black-diamond run, but it was a perfect run for her. She knew she wasn't ready for any black-diamond skiing after the time when she thought she might be ready, turned to look at the mountain while standing perfectly still, and fell. But after seven seasons of skiing, she finally made that one special run that stayed in her memory. She was determined to make it to the bottom without stopping. The run began with an initially steep descent where she slowly and cautiously made her way to a blending with another run that was more familiar to her. She hadn't stopped yet and felt a rush as she began the next descent on a broader groomed slope. She was feeling cocky and even looked for some mini mounds where she might jump and get some air. She found one that would make any experienced skier look at her like she was a complete fool – she didn't care. From the wide-open-groomed slope, the run narrowed and she tossed the idea around in her head as to whether or not she would attempt the short black-diamond run that veered off to the right. Why not? No groomed run there. It was powdery in a thick mushy sort of way. Her knees were definitely burning by then but she was determined to keep going. She did make it down that advanced hill and was back on an open semi-groomed hill with only a short distance to go before reaching the bottom. She made it. Another personal achievement in her life was added to the list. She was elated and headed to the lodge for a hot chocolate topped with whip cream to be savored in front of a roaring fireplace. Was she satisfied? No. Maybe her worth had nothing to do with accomplishments.

Labor Day weekend was the annual arts and crafts festival on Catalina Island and was something she always enjoyed attending. It also benefited her to head south from Avalon as she would be far enough off shore for a good point of sail for the second leg of the trip. Maybe she could find some kind of token from among the many artists – a lucky charm of sorts. The harbor was buzzing with boats and people. Catherine was excited to be in the frenzy of the day and eager to get Whispering Spirit settled so she could go ashore. The morning was well underway with a sparkling freshness in the air. The fog had fully dissipated and the sun was shining brightly. After such a sluggish sail she was famished and wanted a big breakfast at a restaurant overlooking the harbor. From that vantage point she could watch all the artisans setting up their arts and crafts that they had worked so hard on all year long in anticipation of this weekend. Avalon is such a picturesque little town. She always enjoyed the walk on the pier and along the harbor to the Grand Casino where she could look at all the boats.

Walking through the rows and rows of arts and crafts was a delightful experience. There is such an amazing amount of talent in the world. But, then again, there are also a lot of artists who maybe think a little more than they ought to about their work. Whew – some of those price tags were steep. Catherine had been looking for just the right painting to go over the bookshelf in the salon. She finally found it later that afternoon, just before she was ready to call it a day. It was a water color of a cat sitting on a white-washed wall in Mexico wistfully looking out to sea. Perfect! It took her one more day luxuriating on American soil before working up the courage to take a deep breath and begin her voyage to another country.

Meditative Prayer

Dear Lord – your love is so immense. We can't even begin to fathom how great your love is for us. But we join our many brothers and sisters who adore you as best we can, with true heart, broken spirit, and yearning immense. Thank you for implanting in your chosen ones the tiny seed that grows and blossoms in season, and sometimes even out of season, but never dies.

Journal Prompt

Inadequate though our love is, do you accept it anyway Lord, with joy? Can you forgive the believer who seeks you, but not whole heartedly as we should? Can you have compassion on the one who hasn't quite figured out how to pray unceasingly?

Chapter 4

SUBSTITUTION

Nightfall was before Catherine as she passed through the invisible gate to a foreign land leaving California and her youth behind. All was peaceful and she was content as she watched the stars blinking into existence. It seemed like she was alone on the vast stretch of ocean unconcerned about boundaries. But then she saw an unusually bright light on the horizon. She watched it manifest itself getting brighter and looming closer with each passing minute. She wondered why the ship wouldn't veer away from her. They seemed to be on a collision course. And then she realized that it was not a ship at all, but a star. Catherine realized she'd been in smoggy Los Angeles for too long. She wasn't used to that kind of clarity.

Muddled confusion followed her everywhere. Why does it take so long to become wise? Do we ever really obtain wisdom? Will each mile, or milestone, that she leaves behind her lead her to wisdom? Or does God cover himself with a semi-transparent veil to ensure that we constantly seek him without indulging in too much independence? Perhaps wisdom is designed for a life that won't come fully into fruition until time as we know it ends and eternity begins. Is eternity our true north star? Maybe Jesus, like Paul, is limiting us to milk instead of solid food because he sees we are not yet ready for real wisdom. Maybe we are too entangled in worldly head knowledge instead of abiding in faith knowledge (1 Corinthians 3:2-3).

Intimate Stranger

Intimate stranger, heart of my heart

Consume me, entangle me

Captain my chart

Lay out my course

Heading toward the north star

For you are my source

And strength for the war

That I have to fight daily

From the evil one's snare

As I look heavenward mainly

To stay in your care

But also to love you

Dear king I adore

Hoping one day I'll call you

A stranger no more

A note about flags is in order here. While in foreign waters Catherine flew the national flag of the country where she was sailing under the starboard spreader. She flew the U.S. flag, the vessel's national flag, on the port side. Every night she took the flags down before the sun set unless she was entering or leaving port. Before going ashore for the first time in a foreign country, she initially flew the yellow quarantine "Q" flag until being cleared by customs and immigration for entry into the country.

It was early morning and Whispering Spirit was anchored off Islas de Todos Santos. The anchorage was a little exposed, so Catherine's eggs would be scrambled. The gimbaled stove does a nice job of helping her with this task. After breakfast she decided to head over to Ensenada so she could go ashore and find some fresh produce for the next leg of the trip. She got the Avon ready to be lowered over the side when all of a sudden she saw with a fright something about the size of Whispering Spirit in the water.

Catherine's breath was taken from her when she realized there was a whale right next to the hull. It was so close she could almost reach over the side and touch it. This beautiful gray leviathan sensed her nearness and rolled on its side as curious about her as Catherine was about it. They stared at each other in fascination for a mere moment in time. Inside Catherine was so excited she was ready to burst. Then all too quickly the Lord of the Sea disappeared. It was as if God was letting her know that he was near and that no harm would come to her on this crazy excursion.

Just like the hawk, the whale seemed to be yet another messenger from God. These creatures took on spiritual qualities, like guardian angels. And then she began to wonder. Were these creatures a substitute until she was ready to meet Jesus face to face? Catherine wasn't quite ready to let God love her because she hadn't yet fully accepted that he even could love her. She wasn't ready to allow Christ to die for her sins. In attempting to hold on to her pride (her shame?), she needed Jesus to see that she was also bleeding. As she slowly crawled toward the cross, her filthy rags were her badge of honor. She wanted Jesus to see that she was dying along with him.

AUTUMN

So beautiful, in dying, in death

All the colors of the soul, finally released

Beauty hidden, fearful, at last brought forth, for all to see

Green leaves, supple and green, too young for song

Dying leaves, crisp with age, staccato rhythms, with the wind and rain

Glistening dew drops on frosty morn, poised to fall

captured by the dawn's light, unhurried, clinging tenaciously, like pride

Gentle breeze embraces dignity, encouraging the freedom

to release, to trust, to soar, to float, to fall

Barren branches of autumn, nothing hidden, soul on display

Asleep until a new season erupts, and begins the cycle again

Catherine was the evil one hanging next to Jesus on her own cross of despair.

But Jesus refuses to play fair. He refused to look away in disgust. Catherine wondered why Jesus wouldn't see her as she really was. She couldn't look at him. She refused to be pulled into his magnetic gaze. The creatures he was sending her way were easier to acknowledge in her stubbornness. Catherine yearned for the covering of night so she could hide from him. The polarization was too confusing for her. She disliked herself intensely for all the sins she'd committed against others, but mostly for the sins that ravaged her own soul. Her journey was an attempt to sail away from her past. Catherine wanted to be pure again and leave all her ugliness behind her. She wanted to love and be loved in a holy union. She wanted a second chance to get it all right. She wanted to be reborn, cleansed, and made new. She found it impossible to believe that this was even remotely possible. So she got the chart out for her next destination and got underway.

Meditative Prayer

Oh Father, thank you for the seasons of our lives. Thank you for being there on the other side of sadness turned to joy, of defeat turned to conquering success, and of emptiness to fullness at the acknowledgement of your love.

Journal Prompt

What season are you in now? If times are hard, can you see the light of Jesus at the end of your tunnel? If you are in a season of triumph, are you acknowledging Jesus with prayers of thanksgiving?

Chapter 5

UNWELCOME VISITORS

OK, her nerves are fully rattled. Catherine was powering along minding her own business waiting for a breeze to come up just a little bit more so she could set the sails, when a Mexican Navy ship came alongside and started waving some flags at her. She quickly ran below to grab her book about sailing and discovered that they wanted her to heave to and prepare to be boarded. Four men armed and in uniform came alongside the swim ladder that she'd put over the side for them and one of them boarded Whispering Spirit. Formal pleasantries were exchanged in Spanish as he began to search every nook and corner of the boat. When he saw the shotgun in the hanging closet, Catherine thought he might have something to say about that, but he plainly ignored it and kept searching. Leaving behind scuff marks from his black-soled shoes on Whispering Spirit's clean white deck was the only real offense of his short visit. Of course he didn't find any drugs and they went on their serious way to seek out other would-be pirates lurking in their territory.

The wind came up and her anxiety from their boarding went down. It was time to unfurl the jib, hoist the main, and say a prayer of thanksgiving. The day was glorious and Catherine felt giddy as the sun shone and the wind blew a steady breeze enjoying another perfect sail.

A curious thing happened while trolling. Catherine managed to catch a tiny mackerel which she pan fried for dinner. But the tiny octopus she caught next created a lump in her throat at any pain she might have caused this adorable little creature. She hurriedly unhooked it and released it to its home in the watery depths. No pardon for the mackerel, but full release for the octopus. Catherine guessed that we all get to play judge and jury in our daily deliberations. She prayed God would be kinder to her than she was to the mackerel come judgment day.

Catherine's next stops were first San Quintin and then Geronimo Island. San Quintin afforded her a peaceful night's sleep with calm seas. With the morning's stillness, she decided to power over to Geronimo Island. She was almost parallel to the surf breaking when the engine died. The small forward tank was empty. It took some frantic minutes to bleed the air out of the engine before she could run it again using fuel from the big tank. Whew! She really didn't enjoy that kind of scare coming. Keeping more distance from the shoreline in the future would be wise.

Landlubbers might be perplexed to think of the land as being problematic for sailors. But it often causes even more danger. The safest place for a boat to be in a storm is out to sea, not close enough to land to risk being ship wrecked. Sometimes Catherine wondered about being close to Jesus. There were times when she didn't want Mr.-Know-All-See-All to be aware of what she was doing, or thinking, or feeling. She did have the option of turning away from him and doing her own thing, but at what cost? It's a boundary issue Catherine believes. She would rather he establish her limits and then do what she could to be obedient. After a while, he wouldn't even need to display the big stick because obeying will just get easier with habit. She knew there was nowhere she could go to hide from him anyway, so delving into obstinate intentional sin is futile.

Meditative Prayer

Heavenly Father, it's your love that keeps us on the straight and narrow. OK. Admittedly, fear also helps us to want to be obedient. You've brought so many of us such a long way. Please help us when we slip and fall. Please don't let our skinned knees keep us from getting on those same bruised knees to seek you in prayer very quickly.

Journal Prompt

What is foreign that creeps into our lives and tantalizingly seeks to have us forsake the one who loves us? With God's help gazing lovingly upon us, we can turn quickly from the sin that beckons. Remorse and repentance get easier with time spent daily in the Bible helping us to quickly turn from danger.

Chapter 6

WHITE CAPS AND DOLPHINS

On the way to Cedros Island the water was so choppy that Catherine lost her balance and dropped a winch handle over the side. She was so glad she had a backup. But she was going to need to get another one. Thank goodness she got her ham license so she could put in patches now and then state side to friends who could help her in situations like this. She arranged it so that a spare winch handle would be waiting at the marina in Cabo San Lucas.

Catherine got a general class ham license. Oh well. Other than the popularly known dit-dit-dit-dah-dah-dah-dit-dit-dit, she struggled remembering any Morse code. But knowing the code for Save Our Ship (S.O.S.) might come in handy someday if she should happen to find herself in an emergency. Hopefully not, but one never knows. Her rig was an Atlas 215X with a transmitter output of 200 watts and a long wire antenna; i.e., the backstay. She was running barefoot, meaning she did not have an amplifier. She typically used two radio sites; the Mañana Net at 14340 which she often tuned into at 1300 CST, and the Pacific Maritime Net at 14313. Sometimes it was challenging to find a clear frequency within the band limits for chatting with someone more privately, but it is essential to maintain radio etiquette and keep certain frequencies clear for emergency communications.

Catherine became increasingly aware of her arrogance shrouded in insecurity. Her escape to sea was an attempt to run away from herself, as if that were even possible. How could she find Jesus if she was all caught up in her own pride? How do mere mortals become holy? She prayed for God to guide her course into obedience to his plans for her life and to help her overcome her stubborn nature. Why couldn't she just accept that salvation was so easily offered? Why did she argue with God about a gift he wanted her to have? There was too much anger seething deep within her soul about past injustices. How could she rid herself of these memories, or at least find peace with them? When she finally returned to society, she longed to return whole, healthy, and ready to give as well as receive with a gracious spirit. More importantly, she wanted her life to have purpose and meaning. She knew she could no longer tolerate just working an 8 to 5 job and then killing time in front of the television. Catherine wanted the fight beaten out of her so she could learn how to love, really love, deeply and passionately – and in purity. She was holding on to too much bitterness. She needed release from her pent-up anger. She needed to find a way to forgive. Wasn't it easier for God to forgive? After all, he's all powerful. Catherine knew she was just a poor slob trying to make her way in a world that too often seemed unkind. Like a recalcitrant child, she didn't want to forgive those who hurt her. But she wanted to be forgiven. What a conundrum!

All afternoon the wind had been getting stronger and the white caps more prevalent. Catherine partially rolled in the jib furling and was ready to reef the main. In that kind of sloppy sea she was glad to have devised her life vest to have two lines with hooks to keep her tethered to the boat at all times, especially when going forward on the deck. With one hook on the mast and one on the life line she felt more secure reefing the main. She sailed for a couple of hours at six knots with only a partially furled jib and reduced main. The wind was a blustery 35 knots. There was a following sea and the wind was on the stern, so she decided to vang the boom over to one side. She wasn't feeling very good about a rubberized preventer and would get that replaced as soon as possible. Each lift of the stern was causing the boom to strain and try to break free of its constraints. The next vang would be a non-rubberized one to firmly keep the boom in place.

Now that the visibility had been reduced with the onset of evening, Catherine's hearing had become quite acute. She could hear the swell of a following sea approaching even before it was under her. As the rolling wave lifted the stern, Whispering Spirit was propelled forward and it felt like a roller coaster ride surfing at eight knots. As the white capping of the sea slapped the hull, a fine mist of spray splashed over the gunnels and into the cockpit. With a following sea the spray was having sport with the back of her neck. The only way to escape getting splashed was to go below decks, and Catherine was too unsettled to do that just yet. So she went deeper into a pity party and just slugged through until morning. No cat naps that night. She remained too alert with fear wondering if the weather was going to get even worse.

The only trip below decks that harrowing night was to visit the head. There's a reason why the heads onboard sailboats are so small. You need to be able to balance yourself in rough seas by pushing your hands against the bulkheads. Otherwise you risk being thrown out of the saddle. The head can be quite the bronking buck in inclement weather.

Why does it seem that we pray more often when we are scared? Oh Creator of the Universe, did you create times like this to entice us to call out to you? Catherine was confident he didn't take pleasure in the fear of his children, but she did wonder if he ever got so lonely that he allowed times like this as a reason to share in our fear. Her nerves were on edge. It was dark and the sea was not happy – or maybe it didn't care – it just is what it is. She knew Jesus could calm any storm so she prayed for him to calm the storm she was in. Or maybe a better request was asking that he stay close to help her just get through the trial. Catherine was not as strong as she often pretended to be. Right then she was more than aware of her frailties and desperately needed to know that her Captain was near. There was no way she would be able to sail in this storm alone.

She couldn't help but commiserate as to why she was on this crazy trip anyway. What was she doing? Where was she going? Did God send her on this quest, or did she enter into this world of danger and unknown on her own without his Blessing? Abraham had a directive from God to go. Dare Catherine make a claim to that same directive? She needed to trust that God was with her that cold dark night sailing in foreign waters in the middle of a storm. She needed to learn to trust that Jesus was alive and watching over her in any situation, but especially this one.

When Catherine was younger she had an asthma attack so severe that she remembered nothing from the time the paramedics came to her home until she became conscious again three days later. A friend was sitting in a chair by the bedside. She was hooked up to all kinds of paraphernalia but wanted to let her friend know how grateful she was that she was there. The hospital staff had induced medication to keep Catherine immobilized. However, she could shed a tear. That much she could do on her own. Her friend, the Pastor from church, acknowledged Catherine's effort at communicating with her and smiled. Now Catherine understood why people are sure they've seen angels. There was one sitting right next to her. In her heart she thanked her dear friend knowing she could have so easily died. Does God save people from certain death for some grand purpose? Catherine wondered what she could possibly do to be worthy of restored life. Or maybe Jesus had just wanted to give her a chance to fully acknowledge him as her savior before it was time to die for real.

The dawn was almost perceptible. Catherine was exhausted. She thought she could see some light starting to show. Unless she was going mad, there was a strange sound that she kept hearing in addition to the sound of the wind-tossed waves. She heard a splashing sound that was out of sync with all the other noises that had become all too familiar. As the dawn began to break, she was beginning to see how tumultuous the sea really was with white capping crests stretching as far as the horizon. But at least she could finally see and that made a huge difference, although at that moment she couldn't really detect if it was for better or worse.

And now Catherine knew what was making the splashing sounds. There were about a dozen porpoises accompanying her as they played around the boat. She started laughing so hard to the point of hysteria. These creatures were so beautiful! She cautiously inched her way forward to the bow where she could watch them as they raced with Whispering Spirit. She leaned through the pulpit and reached out to them as they surfed, jumped, and dove through the bow's waves in rhythm with the forward bouncing momentum of the boat. Fear was vanishing as she watched them with their antics jumping high in the air and then splashing in the water. They were having so much fun. Did Heavenly Father send them? It was comforting to Catherine knowing that he never did leave her side. But since she was too ignorant to recognize his presence he sent her those lovely new friends. Catherine thanked her new acquaintances. It was almost like they were speaking to her in their high-pitched squeals saying "don't worry – don't worry – don't worry. He watches over you just like he watches over us." Catherine's world was safe again. She thanked Jesus and told him he could go back to sleep.

Seeing Cedros Island so close with the thought of being safely anchored and getting some badly-needed sleep almost a reality, Catherine didn't even mind the thickening kelp beds threatening entanglement with the prop. She was too drained to succumb to any more nonsense from Mother Nature and determinedly swore at the kelp to stay out of her way as she maneuvered to a protected anchorage on the south side of the island. It couldn't have taken her more than ten minutes to kill the engine after setting the anchor before her head hit the pillow and she slept like a log for many hours. The next dawn brought exquisite beauty and sunshine sparkling like rubies and diamonds on the glistening water reflecting the colors of the morning sky. The slightly rolling swells left over from the storm caught the sun's light as if waltzing for joy under the Father's gaze. Catherine went for a very short swim in the cool still-choppy waters all the while keeping in mind that she needed to maintain modesty with the locals. She felt it important to remain cognizant of cultural norms. It was one thing to go swimming at a touristy hot spot in Mexico, and quite another to be seen in a bathing suit near a rural village. She saw no one and felt refreshed in the water's chilling embrace following such a harrowing night.

After resting for another day to allow her nerves to fully recuperate, Catherine headed for the fuel dock to fill the tanks. Nearing the dock, she was amazed that it was still standing it was so rickety. Thankfully there were quite a few locals there to help her come alongside and tie up safely. The sea hadn't quite settled down and it was tricky trying to hold Whispering Spirit steady as each fender took a battering against the crumbling dock. The poor fenders were no longer pure white. From her sordid past she could relate.

Meditative Prayer

In the vessel, you changed the water into wine performing your first public miracle. In a sailing vessel you calmed the stormy seas and let your disciples know that they were protected all along. In the vessel that is our body, you perform many miracles. You open our eyes and let us see that you are within, and that we are safe in your harbor of love.

Journal Prompt

How can we stretch our vision beyond the trouble that looms immediately in front of us knowing calm is just over the horizon? Most of us have favorite Scripture verses to help us find rest in our storms. Help us Lord to memorize that which brings comfort.

Chapter 7

LOOKING UP

After such a frightening couple of days at sea, it didn't matter so much that there was only the merest whisper of a breeze the day of departure from Cedros. And Catherine definitely didn't mind that the sea had seriously calmed down. In fact, it had the appearance of mirrored glass. Another change was the weather. The temperature was steaming in the direct sunlight. The next destination was Puerto Magdalena and she expected to arrive some time the following morning. She could have gotten there sooner if she had cranked up the engine, but she didn't want to waste the diesel. The next fuel dock wasn't until she entered the marina in Cabo San Lucas.

It was a moonless night and the stars were taking their sweet time to come out. As it grew dark, melancholy set in. How Catherine wished she could just erase all the sins that haunted her. Her thoughts soared beyond the halo of the masthead light into the canopy of enveloping darkness. She sensed Jesus' loving gaze. He knew her struggles and she knew he wanted to help. There is promise in looking up. It's interesting to think about why. Maybe it's because that is where we think of heaven being located in the cosmos. And Jesus did say "I am from above" (John 8:23). Just then as if on cue the North Star appeared. Everything was so still. The turmoil battling within her spirit calmed down and the peacefulness felt like a dreamy caress. One star after another appeared displaying its twinkling brilliance. In rapid succession the sky began to illuminate with the starry host and her sadness floated heavenward as Jesus carried her burdens once again. Catherine was reminded that he alone is "the way and the truth and the life" (John 14:6). Heaven is wonder, hope, magic, and reality.

She really enjoyed sailing at night unless the sea was tumultuous. It's very cozy somehow. Catherine liked to pass the time singing. There were small snacks prepared in advance to give her the energy she needed to stay awake. The world looked so different at night. Everything is magnified when the skies are clear. She loved picking out the constellations and thinking about their meaning. Pleiades and Orion were her favorites. She could see the mighty hunter and his attraction to the seven sisters. You can only see Pleiades when you are not looking directly at them. Chasing them must have been very frustrating for Orion. He could never quite hold them in his gaze. Catherine felt the same way when she thought about Jesus. She wanted to simply gaze upon his loveliness for long stretches of time, but the moments pass too quickly and she got easily distracted. Yet she tried so hard to keep him in focus. Why is something so wonderful so difficult? Catherine holds tension in her shoulders. They rise with each new level of stress. She liked to picture Jesus standing before her and gently pushing her shoulders back down, calming her, loving her.

Meditative Prayer

Heavenly Father – How would you have us consider faith? Is it passive and still, or is it alive and seeking, or perhaps it is both? Maybe you would have us reflect upon faith like we do your Son Jesus – now, but not yet.

Journal Prompt

Imagine the stars to be the Heavenly Host. Oh my! So grand for our limited understanding! Yet you are there in our midst. Watching! Loving!

Chapter 8

THE BARTER

It took quite a few more stops before reaching the southern tip of Baja. Most of them, thankfully, were without event. There were quite a few yachties making the same trip and sometimes it felt comforting anchoring alongside them. But sometimes Catherine just wished that she could have anchorages all to herself and not have to bother with being sociable. Puerto Magdalena was a huge inlet bay and she did not have to share it with other yachties while there.

The stillness of the air carried with it a sweltering heat. Thank goodness for the canopy that covered the boom and connected to the lifelines. The dodger alone was insufficient for protection from the sun since it only covered a fraction of the cockpit. Without the canopy covering she would have melted for sure. Seeing a lone fisherman in his *ponga*, Catherine decided to ignore the discomfort of the heat and pay him a visit to see if he might have any fish for trade. From her own *ponga*, she called out to him as soon as she got in calling distance and greeted him in Spanish. "*Buenos Dias Señor. Tiene usted pesca?*" He responded that he didn't have any fish but offered to give her some of his lobster if she was interested. Duh! As an exchange for a bottle of wine she got twenty five lobsters. He tossed them in the front section of the dinghy and Catherine hoped that they would stay put. Imagine twenty five live lobsters crawling around in a tiny inflatable. She couldn't get back to Whispering Spirit fast enough to transfer them onboard and get out of harm's way. After donning some leather gloves each one was tossed into the cockpit.

OK, all aboard. Now what? A cookbook revealed that one way to cook lobster was to bring a very large pot of water to boil and then drop them in one by one until they're cooked. Right! Unfortunately, the lobsters weren't in agreement with this plan. After getting the first one in, he or she somehow grabbed hold of the side of the pot and started splashing its tail in frantic desperation to get out of the cauldron. Water splashed all over the place. Catherine was frantic because she couldn't stand cruelty to any living creature. In tears Catherine's thoughts raced trying to figure out a way to get the lobster securely into the pot and out of its misery as fast as possible. After what seemed like such a long struggle she finally did succeed in getting it into the water and covered the pot with a lid. One down with twenty four more to go!

That was ridiculous. There had to be a more humane way to cook lobster. While God did give us the right to rule over the animals he created, he did not create us to be cruel. She had an idea. With the leather gloves on, she picked up one of the lobsters and quickly twisted the tail from the body, threw the useless claws of the Pacific lobster back into the sea, and cooked just the tails. Mission accomplished. All those delicious lobster tails were then stored away in the bottom of the top-loading refrigeration locker where they would stay frozen until ready to enjoy them for several wonderful dinners. What a treat! She gave thanks to God for his abundant provisioning!

It was Christmas and Catherine was alone. If it weren't for the lobster fest she'd be feeling pretty depressed. She did get a patch into her family for an exchange of holiday greetings. It was times like this when solitude wasn't such a joyful thing. She was reminded of all the family gatherings around a Christmas tree enjoying each other's company and giving thanks at meal time for the turkey, mashed potatoes, sweet potatoes, green beans, and razzleberry sauce. Then thoughts of Jesus on the cross came to mind and how alone he must have felt. But this was Christmas, a time to think about Jesus' birth, not his death. It's so difficult to comprehend a love so great that Jesus would leave Heaven to share such wonderful good news with a sinful creation so that we could be presented clean before the Father. And Jesus made it so simple. In Acts 16:30-31 a prison guard asked

"…what must I do to be saved?" And Paul and Silas answered "…Believe in the Lord Jesus, and you will be saved…" thereby comforting believers that it's not our works that save us. Catherine knew that her belief was growing stronger. But she was also still so drawn to that Scripture verse where someone cried out for Jesus to help him with his unbelief. Jesus has compassion for our struggle. That's why he also gave us the verse "Now faith is confidence in what we hope for and assurance about what we do not see" (Hebrews 11:1).

Meditative Prayer

Father God, forgive us when we stoop to bartering with you. Isn't it childish to keep making promises that we know we won't keep? We promise to stop doing that.

Journal Prompt

What cauldron are you splashing around in today? How can you put a lid on it?

Chapter 9

MIRA! CABO SAN LUCAS

Look! Cabo San Lucas, the Cape of Saint Luke! Finally! After being at sea for what seemed a long time, Catherine couldn't wait to round the bend into deliciously consistent comfortable temperatures and calmer water (or so she thought at the time). The blue Pacific isn't as pacifying as one would think by the name. It would take at least a week in the marina to get caught up on all the chores. Best of all was looking forward to a fresh-water shower. Those salt-water baths were ok; but fresh water – now that was a luxury she never thought she'd call a luxury. Shopping in a touristy town is fun for a little while too, but Catherine was much happier being anchored in a quiet cove somewhere, so it was important to stay focused on the work at hand in order to shove off as quickly as possible.

The next day was set aside for play with an excursion in the dinghy out to the point. Between the jagged rocks you can walk from calm serenity to the turmoil of the Pacific Ocean in just a few steps. The sea seemed to reflect Catherine's own emotions that consistently vacillated between calm and unrest. The surf on the Pacific side was pounding on the beach and was much too treacherous to enter for a swim. As she walked along she saw a tiny bird sitting quietly just ahead of her in the sand. She approached it but it wouldn't fly away. How strange. She picked it up very tenderly and breathed gently on its wings thinking that might help somehow. It did. The bird flew away a few seconds later.

God speaks in so many wondrous ways. Like that sweet little sparrow seemingly being healed by human breath Catherine felt nourished as if Holy Spirit had just breathed upon her as well. We are so blessed to have moments like that to be at one with God. It was time to leave the non-pacifying ocean and retrace her footsteps to the stillness of quieter waters. Isn't Jesus always just a breath away? Catherine needed some reflection time to simply be present with God. He made us for fellowship with him. Catherine hated being ignored and she couldn't even begin to imagine Jesus' pain at being ignored when he's always by our side.

Spending quiet time with Jesus was rejuvenating and instilled a desire to commune with his creation by snorkeling around the rocky point. Slipping into the water, she ventured out a little way to be in the sunshine outside of the shade of the cliff. All of a sudden she was surrounded by hundreds of tiny little fish. Her first sensation was that of fear. She was in the midst of a sea of brilliant colors and flashing movement. She decided to relax and pretended to be a fish herself. What an incredible experience. It was like being a member of their school and they were learning about me. The sun's rays were filtering through the clear blue of the water and sparkling on the shiny scales of so many fish darting all about. It felt like being surrounded by an army protecting her from any outside intruders, and it was glorious. Later she would paint a water color of that moment.

Before heading back to Whispering Spirit she rowed the dinghy over to the immense rock formations that are so picturesque just south of the two-sided beach. After that incredible snorkeling experience she wanted to see what the area looked like from on top of the water. The natural arch formation was amazing to see up close. A colony of seals languorously barked their delight at the ticklish sea spray. With no one in hearing distance Catherine joined their choir and sang at the top of her lungs. She hoped their discordant melody brought a smile to the heavenly host before they hurried to plug up their ears. Even Sophia runs and hides when she sings.

Back on board Whispering Spirit she searched the Scriptures remembering that there was something about birds and found what she was looking for in Matthew 10:29-31 "Are not two sparrows sold for a penny? Yet not one of them will fall to the ground outside your Father's care. And even the very hairs of your head are all numbered. So don't be afraid; you are worth more than many sparrows." Catherine asked the Father if he sent that little sparrow to wait for her to show her that she has worth in his eyes.

Meditative Prayer

Like you care for the sparrow, help us to know that we are in your care precious Lord. Oh to be still, and just know.

Journal Prompt

What prompts you to know that Holy Spirit is near? Can you feel his presence in a gentle breeze? Does it take lightning and thunder for you to experience his power? When are you aware that YOU have the power of Holy Spirit?

Chapter 10

CHORES GALORE

There was so much to do. Washing clothes at the local *lavamatica* meant getting to wear clean clothes that weren't stiff and salty. But it meant hauling all the dirty laundry into town and then waiting and watching blindly mesmerized by the twirling cycle of clothes in the machine. With no dryers in Mexico – at least none that she had found so far – Catherine then had to carry heavy wet clothes back to Whispering Spirit. There was no opportunity for modesty when all the clothes were hanging on the life lines to dry. Everyone gets to see what kind of panties you wear while they're flying like a flag in full view. At least she got to sort of hide behind them in the cockpit. Thankfully no one mistook them for an invitation to social hour. If she had hoisted them up the aft stay it would have definitely sent the wrong message. Thankfully with the dry heat they dried quickly and the embarrassment passed soon enough.

In addition to finding the Post Office to pick up the new spare winch handle, it was sweet to read letters from home. Family and friends always knew where to send letters for that next port of call in a city that had an *Oficina de Correos*. Next stop was to find the *banco* in order to exchange some American dollars for Pesos. Purchasing a fishing permit allowed one month of legal fishing. Checking in with the Port Captain and *Immigracion* was no small feat since they are located so far apart from each other. The last item on the to-do list was to get some gas for the outboard. It might seem like overkill having two dinghies, but they each served a valid purpose. The hard dinghy with the outboard was very useful when anchored in a location where it was necessary to go a long way to get some place. The soft dinghy kept on the foredeck was super easy to toss over the lifelines using just the oars to get around.

Shopping for food in a Mexican town was fun and could be quite different from shopping in good old Estados Unidos (U.S.). In Mexico it was normal to shop at several markets for each different kind of item. Catherine's absolute favorite was the *panaderia*. She didn't even need to ask directions but just followed her nose to the heavenly smell of baking bread early in the morning. Mexican bread is not sweet like some of the kinds you might buy in a bakery in the States. To buy meat was a little trickier. Memories were fresh when shopping at a *carniceria* where the cow had just been slaughtered in the back yard and brought in for sale. With no refrigeration in many of the rural markets, it was important to purchase freshly butchered meat. You could also buy chickens that had only recently had their necks wrung and still had a few lingering feathers yet to be plucked clinging to their skin. Someone advised that soaking vegetables in iodine acts as a safeguard to prevent you from getting the *turistas*. It really didn't matter if this was an old wives' tale because Catherine was willing to do whatever it took to try and keep from getting sick.

With all the easy stuff taken care of, it was time to go to the fueling dock and fill the tanks with both diesel fuel and water. Fortunately this particular dock was inside a marina and the water was calm. Fueling up at a dock like the one at Cedros Island can get really scary. It took a long time to fill the 70-gallon water and fuel tanks. The super tricky part was then adding just the right amount of bleach to purify the water for safe drinking. She added too much once and nearly burned her throat.

Cabo is such a quaint little town. One morning Catherine invited a parrot to sit on her shoulder while enjoying breakfast at a little outdoor restaurant on the beach. Maybe this colorful little winged creature was really an angel in disguise. But when it nipped her ear she changed her mind and disinvited it as a potential friend. Not everything beautiful is good for us. Catherine decided to ignore the tanned hunk staring at her from the other table.

She shouldn't have spent the money but decided to splurge on an evening of wine, delicious food, and music at the *Finnestere* located high on a cliff overlooking the Pacific Ocean. It was almost her birthday and she wanted to spoil herself a little. As a leap-year baby she didn't often get to have a real birthday. This was one of those not-on-the-calendar birthday years but she wanted to celebrate anyway. The setting sun over the blue Pacific from this hilltop bit of paradise was exquisitely colorful this lovely evening. With her well-developed tan, long hair, and fancy/casual dress, Catherine actually felt pretty. Hey, every woman should have moments when she feels like she looks good, especially on her special day. It's good for the soul. Too bad she was such a loner. Someday she hoped to change that and fall deliciously in love with a man who follows Jesus; but that time seems like it's on the distant horizon. Sigh!

There was no reason not to head out the next day so Catherine left for an anchorage just around the corner called Chileno where the Hotel Cabo San Lucas is located. This anchorage ranked high as one of the more beautiful places she'd anchored thus far. The water was a heavenly shade of bluish green and so clear it was hard to tell the distance to the bottom. One day she put on a sun dress to visit the hotel's restaurant and rowed ashore. When she was ready to get out and pull the dinghy up on the beach she misjudged where the bottom was and got out a tad too early. The water came up to her neck. So much for the pretty dress! She was drenched and thoroughly embarrassed and had to row back to the boat and find another dress and figure out if a repeat of the exercise was worth it. She decided to leave her pride behind and ventured out again. The eating area of the restaurant had no windows, a *palapa* roof, and looked out over the ocean. What that meant was that everyone saw Catherine get a dunking. A few of the guests chuckled as she entered the restaurant. She laughed with them and ordered a margarita to wash down the embarrassment. There was a mariachi band playing and she was in the mood for simply and deliciously enjoying life.

Catherine was deliriously happy there. It was so peaceful except when the mariachis were playing, but she really enjoyed the happy-sounding music. She was starting to get adjusted to the cruising life.

Mornings were her favorite time of day. She loved having coffee in the cockpit and watching the sun rise. The following morning she cooked a full breakfast with eggs, bacon, salsa, and avocado wrapped in a tortilla. Yummy!

The morning routine consisted of reading the Bible, studying Spanish for about an hour, then reading some kind of technical journal that was more than likely on engine maintenance or refrigeration while trying not to fall back to sleep. She loved her Bible with the study guide. It gave her insights that she might not have otherwise discovered on her own. Having the time to be disciplined in this way fulfilled the achiever in her.

With the water so clear it was a good opportunity to spend some time scrubbing the hull. A mask and snorkel is probably not the most efficient way to do this but it was the only way in which she was comfortable. She had no desire to own scuba gear – too chicken. She knew claustrophobia would set in and arouse panic. So she took a deep breath and dove and scrubbed as much as she could before floating to the surface for a breath and then doing it all over again until her energy was spent.

It was time for Sophia to have another swimming lesson. She was not going to be very happy about this but it was an essential part of her lifestyle for being so lucky as to live aboard a boat. She argued about that but she was not the boss, and it was for her own good. A rope ladder hung from the base of one of the mid-ship lifelines and descended about three feet below the water line. Before her swimming lesson Sophia's nails were clipped in order to save Catherine's own tender skin. Her nails were clipped regularly and Sophia was typically very cooperative as lavish praise was given with each nail clipped. Tolerant was probably a better word for this process. Before climbing down the swim ladder Catherine wrapped Sophia tightly in a towel – an added safeguard to protect herself from being scratched. When they were in the water Catherine unwrapped the towel and let Sophia swim, all the while guiding her to the rope ladder. She grabbed it for dear life and successfully climbed aboard and raced to the V-berth where she spent the next half hour ferociously tongue drying herself off while attempting to regain her dignity. If she ever accidentally fell overboard Catherine had some measure of confidence that Sophia would be able to get back onboard. Normally she stayed below decks when the sun was out because it hurt her eyes. Nighttime was when she got brave and explored topsides, especially when at anchor and the engine wasn't running. She's so beautiful with her black fur and reddish highlights. Catherine knew she wanted a black cat when she visited the animal shelter. The most beautiful long-haired black cat was crouched in the back of her cage when Catherine saw her and it was love at first sight. She'd do anything to protect her and keep her safe, healthy, and contented.

Bathing was an interesting feat on a sailboat. Every drop of water that went into Whispering Spirit was often put in by the sweat of her brow, so it was precious and needed to be used sparingly. The first step in the bathing process was to jump into the water and get wet, after remembering to put down the swim ladder. Once Catherine forgot and suffered humiliation by having to swim to a nearby boat for help in getting back onboard. To continue the bathing process, after she got wet she climbed back aboard and lathered up with some special soap meant for salt water bathing that was developed to protect the environment. Then she dove back into the water and got thoroughly rinsed. The last step was pouring half a cup of fresh water on her hair to give it a rinse.

After Sophia's swimming lesson and her own bath it was time for a well-earned siesta. Catherine felt refreshed after an hour's nap and decided to go exploring in the dinghy. Maybe she would even catch a fish as she trolled along near the rocky outcropping.

What a lucky day! She did hook a fish. The male Dorado (dolphin fish) displays incredibly beautiful colors as it is being reeled in. Fishing was still an emotional struggle for Catherine because she couldn't stand harming any of God's creatures. But fishing was a staple diet while sailing in waters far away from home. The lure that most often brought luck had a metallic body with green and yellow colored rubbery fins. Death came quickly for her catch and she now had the most delicious dinner to look forward to that evening. A little squirt of lime and some cilantro added to the pan-seared Mahi

Mahi, and voila!

This was such a perfect day. Catherine felt so blessed. She found that she was often giving thanks to God for watching over her and allowing her to experience such an amazing journey. Some day she was going to need to get back into the real world, but not for a little while longer. As night fell, one of her favorite things to do was enjoy a glass of wine while sitting on the boom in the relative cool of the evening. From that vantage point she could admire the purple mountain majesty of the hills of Baja. Sometimes the cockpit felt too confining. Sitting on the boom made her feel like she was more a part of the great outdoors.

Before going to bed she spent some quality time with Sophia who liked to snuggle up next to Catherine on the divan. Her soft breathing and rhythmic purring had a calming effect. This precious gift from God meant a great deal to Catherine. Life is such a miracle. Sometimes Catherine held her hand over her heart and felt her pulse and pictured her heart pumping life into her body. Our blood is our sustenance. And Jesus' blood gives us eternity. Catherine believed God is the creator of life and is involved in every miniscule decision. She didn't know if creation took place over the kind of twenty-four-hour day that we are accustomed to or if creation took billions of years. All she knew is that God created.

One day Catherine wanted to find her true partner in life. She felt confident he was out there. Maybe she already knew him. The song from Fiddler on the Roof comes to mind, "for Papa – make him a scholar, for Mama – make him rich as a king, for me, well, I wouldn't holler if he were as handsome as anything." What a silly song. Catherine's mother always taught her that the most important quality in a spouse is a sense of humor. Her father had that gift so she understood what that meant. Catherine's father was happiest when his family was laughing. Catherine hoped her mate would be smart as well as silly. Without any doubt he would be beautiful in her eyes no matter what he looked like. She just hoped he found her worthy. Darn, that worthy thing wouldn't leave her alone. Maybe Jesus will want her to love him alone for the rest of her life. Catherine knew that Jesus found her worthy. His Word said so. But he also admonishes and encourages us to love one another. Knowing he is a jealous God, she prayed that he would teach her how it is possible to love a man and love him at the same time. She vowed never to make a man an idol but was terribly guilty of putting men on a pedestal. And then there's Adam and Eve – made gloriously beautiful in the potter's hands to love one another and to love God in his heavenly garden. Jesus created a husband and a wife to be united and to cherish each other. Maybe that kind of love wasn't meant for her. She pondered what Jesus meant when he said that "At the resurrection people will neither marry nor be given in marriage…" (Matthew 22:30). It sounded like he was talking about the future; but what about the past carrying over into the future? What if love, as we know it here on earth, will be so gloriously perfect in eternity that Jesus has no way of describing it with our limited understanding? Was she guilty of making Scripture fit into her own cherished notions and desires? She hoped not and often asked forgiveness.

Meditative Prayer

Dear Lord, why do you love us? What have we done to earn your love? It is so easy to feel unworthy. Once in a great while we think we might have done something good to make you pleased with us. Then we laugh at our silliness. Yet, to look at a precious child or pet that we love for no particular reason at all can make us think that this is what it must be like for you with us.

Journal Prompt

How do you fuel up? What fills your tank with the serenity of Christ?

Chapter 11

LOS FRAILLES – Musical Anchorages

Los Frailles is a jut of land sticking out with space to anchor on both the south and the north side in the Sea of Cortez of the Baja Peninsula. Catherine arrived in the late afternoon and dropped the hook on the south side. The wind was howling and is famous for doing exactly that for yachties trying to make their way north up the coastline in the Sea of Cortez. She was so glad to be tucked behind the high hill and protected from the wind. She got in as close as she thought safe and let out plenty of scope on the anchor. Dusk came and silhouetted the distant mountains with the most beautiful hues of pink and purple.

Thinking that she was safely tucked in for the night she slept soundly until she heard the wind pick up. Disturbed, she went out in the cockpit. The wind had done an about face and Whispering Spirit was now swinging on the anchor so that the bow was working its way around to being pointed into the wind. That meant Whispering Spirit was drifting toward the base of the mountain and into shallower waters. It was time to crank the engine and get into deeper water. Catherine wasn't sure what to do next. On a moonless night it seemed like the smartest thing for her to do was to gently nudge her way around to the other side of the jettison of land to find protection from the wind shift. She safely made her way and dropped the anchor and let out a reasonable amount of scope. By then she was too restless to go back to sleep so she just sat in the cockpit waiting for dawn. Wouldn't you know it – the wind began shifting again. Unbelievable!

She was tired, angry, and felt like Mother Nature was messing with her head. She had no choice but to repeat her exercise in futility and drive the boat back around to the other side. She wasn't comfortable with sailing at night when she wasn't in open water. It was nearly dawn and she couldn't wait to get underway again and far away from this goofy place.

Catherine was dizzy from the confusion of the night. Not knowing which anchorage was safe reminded her of her inner turmoil. For years she suffered with feeling like she was never good enough. Too much criticism caused her to doubt her own worth. Back and forth her emotions tumbled around feeling confident one moment and completely insecure the next. She got a Bachelor's Degree and then a Master's Degree. Wasn't she "good enough" after these achievements? Darn demon wouldn't leave her alone.

Writing poems were an avenue of release for her. She wrote to process her thoughts. She felt much better at writing than speaking.

Catherine knew what it meant to have a desolate heart, so perhaps that made her a viable authority on the subject. Why must matters of the heart be so complex and mystifying? Why can't it be as simple as one's soul opening up to the beloved's soul? And if there is no response, why can't the beloved ever so tenderly simply close the window allowing innocent dignity to remain somehow intact?

Catherine did fall deeply and truly in love once and couldn't help but wonder – did she love him more because he loved her not? Was all the pain and suffering worth it? Oh yes! Most definitely yes!

Even so far away from home on a small sailboat in unfamiliar waters Catherine couldn't seem to escape her broken heart. His memory followed her wherever she went. She loved him well but was in it alone and felt betrayed. Yet even so she trusted God enough to know that he knew both of their hearts, and their differences, and that he lovingly chose to say no in answer to her petitions. Fantasies can be so deliciously fulfilling and frustratingly empty at the same time. But for the very first time in her life, she knew what it meant to love someone in purity. Perfection cannot manifest itself in this life, but nobility perhaps has a chance.

Desolate Heart

Ever in your shadow

Never in your light

Forsaken behind a misty clearing

Just shy of grasping truth

You cage your victims carelessly

While demons hold you tight

Let loose the pain that chains

And see with unfeigned eyes

The one who traipses faithfully

With a hopeless desolate heart

Catherine wondered how many wounds she ignored because she never felt worthy of seeking help. She never really took her pain as seriously as it deserved. She was too tough, or so she thought. She never saw herself as important enough to invest in her own healing. By abandoning herself to the whimsies of the wind in a small sailboat she was finally taking steps toward beginning that process. How desperately disparaging it can be to feel unworthy! God created us to think better of ourselves than that. She must find solace in Jesus if she couldn't find refuge in herself.

It was time to pause for some love poems. Love has a mystical way of creating things that are not as though they are. If she lost the memories it would mean losing a part of who she was. Painful though it was for then, she wouldn't change a minute of the moments she had spent with him. It was a time of her life when she was genuinely happy. Of the many definitions Webster has for the word love, the one that applied to Catherine's emotions was the one that defined love as "a deep and tender feeling of affection for or attachment or devotion to a person…" (Webster, 1984, p. 838). With this definition, she could definitely qualify her emotions as love. Tender feelings – check. Affection – check. Devotion – check.

Was she clinging to the wrong vine? God had to prune her in order for her branch to be fruitful. When she was released, there was Jesus, the one who never left her, and the one who never would leave her. It's not that we shouldn't seek love. But there are priorities. If she always made sure Jesus came first, then her life's decisions would be in the correct order.

Catherine couldn't help but wonder when reading the Scripture verse Luke 10:39 about Mary sitting at the Lord's feet listening to all he had to say, if she was ever confused about her love for him? Was her heart stirred gazing upon Jesus the Christ wondering about Jesus the man? Catherine wanted Jesus to teach her how to love him and prayed.

Although this was written for romantic love, Catherine couldn't help but think of Jesus when she pondered the words. How many times did Jesus plainly tell his followers his fate? They heard him

To Love From a Distance

Is not the event made more sacred and dear

in its pain felt sweet remembrance

than in the heat of its occurrence?

And would you deny yourself

the bittersweet torment of a thirst unquenched?

but they could not, or would not, understand. It wasn't until after his resurrection that their memories became clear and they began to comprehend. How she longed to see Jesus face to face. He instilled in her an unquenchable thirst that wouldn't be fully satisfied until that day when unfathomable mysteries were finally made clear. But in her heart she did see his face, and that was very dear to her and sufficient for now. Yet she did wonder about her desire for human love and affection. She had no clear understanding for what to do about that longing except to place her trust in God. If he had someone for her, he would make it happen.

Begging Release

O tempest of my longing soul

Return to me the calm you stole

So long ago when dreams were dormant

Then quickened shamelessly by your enchant

You nurtured and fed my starving shell

You tortured me guilelessly in the sweetness of hell

And now it all ends, or begins anew

My expectant nerves are taut as sinew

Begging for release from propriety imprisoning

Gingerly seeking a pardon still questioning

Why must knowledge and wisdom hover so far apart?

Come solace and ease my aching heart

I am a soldier enslaved to freedom

Yet held captive and bound in willing chains

With this tempest near over and longing for rest

Pray beckon me now to Thy lofty nest

SOPHIA

How many times can a heart be broken?

Once, twice, as many as seven?

Nay but seventy seven times forsaken says I

Once for innocence, and often for pride

But the deepest break is courtly

When that pedestal turns human

And the head knows, while the sorrow grows

And SCREAMS *ever so sweetly*

Stick your neck out

Take a risk and play that fool

In this game called love

Then return to the one who is perfect love

And rest from your folly

Now wiser – Sophia

In the dying embers of a once blazing fire

Honesty burns with the ashes

And I am humbled

It's an old, old friend

And I relish the quiet

Where sanity reigns once more

There is no sweeter sound

Than absolute silence

When stillness rules my kingdom

And I'm peaceful once again

Sweet insanity takes such a toll

And I'm spent from the mockery

Of my own imagination

Yet replete from pure exhaustion

If I Should Die Tonight

I love you Father, Jesus, and Holy Spirit

I also love a man

Yet fear entangles this sacred embrace

Forsaking Never Thee My God

For Jesus is the one I love

Above him even more

Confusion reigns as I embrace

This foolish heart of mine

You command us to love

Is your heart not as jealous as mine?

Teach me how to justify

My love for You, my love for him

For so many years you've captured my heart

While my love for him is young

I'm so afraid of a dwindling devotion

Replaced with mortality and flesh

Please teach me Lord

How to love you more

Than this man who has stolen my heart

For I love you Lord

And I love him too

If it takes my death

To protect him from harm

Then take my life dear Lord

But keep him safe

In your arms of love

Then bring him home to me

Sanctity of Hope

I'm willing to be broken as a sacrifice of love

In humble adoration taught by the Master above

My heart rejoices in the sanctity of hope

The act of loving in itself helps me cope

My taut emotions are stretched and ready to burst

From this secretive cage of bars, denying passion is the worst

Surface tingling so futile and unkind

Now find a deeper meaning that is perfectly sublime

Sensual fantasies still exist

But they're so much easier to resist

Outward expressions must find rest

God is putting me to the test

Wisdom seeks his perfect timing

As my love is ever climbing

Toward a glorious unknown

Of passion bursting to be known

Did Jesus die of a broken heart? Dear friends shared this with Catherine and it explained so much. She need never feel alone knowing Jesus suffered all the things she suffered and yet so much more. She believed the Father's heart was broken too that day when his only begotten Son hung on a tree. The Father could not look upon sin. Jesus knew why he had come to earth. He was fulfilling his appointed destiny on the cross. His love for his creation held him there. But the human God, the son of man, was hurting that day. His body suffered incomprehensible torture. At the hour of exchange he also suffered from a heart that was breaking from perceived rejection and abandonment. Not only was Jesus bereft of his friends, but his Father also looked away in his greatest hour. He could not look upon his Son covered in the sins of his children. But Catherine believed the Father's face was covered in tears and his body was racked in sobs of mutual pain. And then it was finished. Jesus had fulfilled his destiny. Night ended and the dawning of a new morning had come. No further sacrifices are needed to atone for sin for those who believe in this ultimate exchange. Jesus paid a lasting one-time price and is restored to his Father's side. He's home. Catherine's appointed hour would come too when he would bring her home to him.

It was easy to understand how many were being misled. Some people want to think that they can know God through their own endeavors. They don't want to acknowledge that sin that will keep them from entering eternity in Heaven. They don't want to release their unconfessed sins to another, and especially not to God. They don't want to believe that another, even Jesus, could have the power to do what they cannot do. Too many people believe that their own definition of goodness is all it takes to make it into Heaven. Pride is a terrible form of bondage. It began with Adam and Eve. They wanted to be God's equal and know what he knows. How foolish our quests can be when we try to elevate ourselves. Only God can ultimately determine our assigned portion in heaven. A mother's love is often great. But even passionate pleas for the beloved sons of thunder could not sway God to grant elevated positions because "these places belong to those for whom they have been prepared by my Father"

(Matthew 20:23). God the Father knows best what's good for his children.

Maybe the next anchorage would provide the solace Catherine was seeking. She was hoping to linger there to rest her body and her aching spirit. The desert had a certain tug on her heart strings. There was a definite beauty in the barrenness of the hills and the surrounding landscape. Gazing into this emptiness had the effect of clearing her head of clutter and narrowing her focus. There was no cluttered confusion here in this desert – just barren landscape. She was alone for a time so that she could be rooted in Christ. He is no longer on that lonely tree. He was here with her. Jesus said that "I am the vine; you are the branches. If you remain in me and I in you, you will bear much fruit; apart from me you can do nothing" (John 15:5). Catherine's hope was that she was on a path to find truth, even as a woman not quite young and not yet old. Think about how long it took the potter to mold Moses into the person he could finally use. God did not look at her wrinkles; he looked at her desire to love him and others through the love he showered on her.

His Hands

Not young

Not old

Coming into my own

Less fear

More confident

Discovering things that God has already known

Less stupid

More wise

Forming ideas that I long to have sewn

My fabric

His hands

Being sculpted in an image whose reflection is a clone

Love more

Not less

Practicing skills He gave me to hone

Hide less

Justify less

Saner now that He is my capstone

The woman I was

Is not who I am

Because of His love, just see how I've grown

Not alone

Developing backbone

His daughter, complex, someone, milestone

Meditative Prayer

Lord Jesus, we love you. Yet often our love feels so inadequate. Do you see through our inadequacies and accept what little we have to offer? Teach us how to love you more. Prepare us unabashedly for that glorious day when love will be revealed in a way we can't even comprehend right now. We long for you. Anything else is held very lightly anymore.

Journal Prompt

What does it mean to be chosen? Why did Jesus choose a little town called Bethlehem to descend from his throne and reside? Why did God choose planet earth out of the vast universe to inhabit his grace? And why, Lord, did you choose me?

Chapter 12

THE *PALAPAS* OF LA PAZ

The *palapas* of La Paz. These words don't really rhyme unless you force them to rhyme, and then they sound funny. *Palapas* are thatched umbrella-like man-made shade providers and can be found in more places than just La Paz. However, even greater than the shade provided by *palapas*, "the Lord is your shade at your right hand" (Psalm 121:5). Jehovah Jireh is always our provider whether under the protective loving gaze of the Son or under the intense heat of the sun.

During leisurely sails, like the one from Punta Arena just beyond Los Frailles heading toward La Paz, Catherine had time to stick her nose into great books. Right then she was enjoying a book about shells. Catherine loved strolling an empty beach and collecting beautiful shells. The beaches of California were well picked over and any shells that managed to find their way ashore were quickly confiscated. But Mexico has an abundance of beautiful shells, especially on the more isolated beaches.

The absolute favorite shell was the pink Murex – so delicate and lined with ruffles. She was Catherine's elegant lady. By contrast the Conch is the king – large and powerful. But she also really loved the Cowry shells – very tiny, shiny, and adorable. She had an Auger and some Whelk shells. To add color, she has an orange and a pink half shell and many others that she's unable to identify. For the most part, Catherine couldn't tell you about the beaches she's wandered collecting shells because her nose always seemed to be pointing down as she hunted for these treasures.

There are so many great authors. Other favorites of hers while on this journey included the writings of James A. Michener, Kahlil Gibran, Leon Uris, Herman Wouk, James Clavell, Gore Vidal, and Taylor Caldwell. It was such a pleasure to read books of her own choosing now that she had completed her formal studies. But as most anyone could attest who has climbed the ladder of higher education, there is intensity in learning that is genuinely pleasurable while demandingly grueling. Writing a thesis that claims some inner part of you is an addictive journey spurning a previously vacant hole that involves an extreme tension bordering between love and hate. You can't wait for it all to be over and yet you somehow almost enjoy the punishment of each new climactic achievement leading up to graduation. Catherine was glad it was over, but she had to confess that she'd be a formal student again in a heartbeat. Now she was her own disciplinarian.

While getting an education at the university, she wrote some poems as a tribute to a professor who she admired greatly. He helped her to grow as a woman beginning her advent into spiritual maturity. She also attributed her passion for writing to him. He opened up a world of words, literature, cultures, and compassion for which she was forever grateful.

It takes time following graduation to digest all that you've learned. The new ideas need to swirl around for a while. Graduation is almost like attending a funeral. You mourn all that appears to be lost and wonder if you've learned anything at all. When someone close to you dies, their memory, after some healing takes place, catches you by surprise. She appreciated more as that time has elapsed all that she learned. Something would happen and she'd smile and think – oh yeah, I know that, I learned that. But what getting a formal education does for you even more is prepare you for being able to take everything to the next level. Catherine sought learning opportunities following graduation to give her opportunities to think on her own. She had finally earned the right to have her own opinion. Her education gave her a foundation. Her graduation opened windows to use what she had learned with a hunger to formulate new ideas.

Growth

Deep in the forest, enveloped by God,

saplings are nourished, and glisten.

Reach for your destiny and grasp with a nod

that vision you've captured within.

Look up fledglings and spread your limbs.

Brush off the cobwebs and let your rings grow wide

now nurtured and fostered in liquid sunshine.

Pitter patter chitter chatter.

Overcome the cacophony and rise to your zenith.

Hues in splendor, love's divine

like rain drops and learners, uniquely designed.

Dripping drumming heartbeat

resounding out in rhythm.

Leave the trunk inscribed and fill the hollows.

Fret not a life saturated in sorrows.

Transfer the dewdrops, for verdancy will mellow

the discordance of knowledge ill gotten.

Stalwart and rugged stand courageous.

Even mustard seed rivals in vigorous pursuit.

See the old growth in splendor

standing regal and wise.

Fear not his drenching of wisdom proffered,

for the day will come for his benediction

when you'll finally stand tall

rendering your own valediction.

Revealed

A wise man fortuitously entered my world.
I had taken the first steps toward freedom.
Now he gently nudges me through the thickly
forested jungle of a past swept under
the verdant carpet of organic muck.
He revealed me to myself.
Advanced in years, tender shoots of new creation
are slowly breaking through the entangled mire.
Once upon a time I hid behind powerful men
and lived in the shadows of obedience.
Now I'm venturing to peak through the foliage
to the terrifying wonder of open uncharted space.
Where does one hide when exposed and assaulted by
the teachings of a great professor?
I've been revealed and stand naked and exposed
in my healing and growth.
The sun is burning off the deadened layers
of scales as I stand in the unknown.

Catherine decided to stop for a few hours at El Limoña on Isla Cerralvo where she got a patch through on the *mañana net* to her family. The *hey-you-almost-a-doctor* member of the family, nicknamed from her earlier days of being fans of the popular TV comedian, has quite an extensive background in the medical profession and she was relying on him for an update on their mother's progress fighting an illness. The time may come when she would have to find a secure anchorage for Whispering Spirit and a cat sitter for Sophia and fly home to be with her. Either that or she would finally say goodbye to this lifestyle, sell Whispering Spirit to some other wanderlust sailor and fly home. But for now her mother was fighting her own good fight and remained cheerful. One Christmas Catherine gave her a lovely pink Bible and it comforted her to know that her mother was being comforted in the arms of our Heavenly Father through the words of his love letters to her.

There's a wonderful long stretch of sandy beach on Isla Cerralvo and Catherine walked to its lighthouse collecting several beautiful shells along the way. Then she tried her luck at fishing off the stern and felt very lucky to have hooked a Sierra which would make for another tasty dinner. There were always plenty of cracker crumbs aboard for pan frying. But that night she decided to make Ceviche since she had some fresh limes, salsa, and an avocado that had just come into perfect ripeness (yes, it was possible to actually look an avocado in the eye again). Sophia loved fresh fish too and it was fun being her champion when something was caught to her liking. Next stop was an anchorage just around the northern tip of La Paz called Puerto Ballandra. The wind was a little too brisk during that passage and she couldn't wait to get anchored. Ugh – what a night! You would think that a rolly anchorage would gently rock you to sleep, but that didn't work for her. She knew she was going to enjoy the calm and protected anchorage of La Paz. But first she had to see up close the amazing rock structure on the beach in Ballandra. It looked like a golf ball sitting on its tee; only it was about twelve feet high. The locals called it mushroom rock. Either way it was an amazing piece of nature's architecture. Did God give us these anomalies just for our pleasure and for his as well at seeing our looks of awe?

Getting into La Paz is tricky when you're on a boat. You have to time the entry just right because of the extreme tides. It was her lucky day. To her starboard was a sailboat laying at an angle in the sand very close to El Mogote, the spit of land that's the reason for a calm anchorage across from the town of La Paz. They didn't seem anxious about being grounded. They waved to each other while the couple on the grounded boat was enjoying lunch waiting for the tide to come back in so they could get on with maneuvering the tricky channel. Sailing can be a very humbling experience to say the least. But this couple didn't seem humiliated at all. They just made the best of an awkward situation. What a great lesson. They laughed at themselves and released the situation to merriment and nachos.

This brought back memories of another situation while anchored in Catalina Island's Cherry Cove. The Harbor Master was sending out warnings on the radio about a Santa Ana wind that was due to hit the island sometime that evening. Those hot dry winds could be quite devastating to boaters. Catherine had three options. She could go around to the other side of the island to Isthmus Cove, or she could head back to Redondo Beach, or she could stay put and weather it out. The latter option seemed best. She was on a mooring wand and decided to drop an additional anchor off both the bow and stern letting out plenty of scope. She buddy boated over with friends and they determined to stick together and hope for the best. As evening set in and the wind was eerily quiet, all the boaters headed off to a pensive sleep. When the wind picked up steam around 1300, all the yachties who had chosen to remain were now very much awake and hanging out in their cockpits. As the wind grew stronger, the water also got quite choppy. Whispering Spirit looked like a bucking bronco horse as she rode the waves charging into the anchorage. Catherine had a good idea what she looked like by watching her friend's boat doing her own bronco ride (boats are often referred to in the female gender). They had a camera and she got to see later just how high Whispering Spirit could jump. When dawn finally broke, they both decided enough was enough and made plans to head home. It would be a miserable sail but perhaps less nerve wracking than riding out the storm tied up and helplessly waiting for the wind to abate. They were close enough to be heard over the wind as they yelled their intentions to each other. Catherine cranked the engine and figured out how she would get untangled from the mooring wand and both anchor lines. She put the engine in forward and slowly moved up on the bow anchor and brought it on board. The automated anchor system made that job a piece of cake. Then she began the arduous task of pulling the stern anchor on board. With that stowed away, all that was left was to release the mooring wand. She waited what seemed like a reasonable amount of time; but with the water so choppy it was difficult to see if the line had actually dropped. It hadn't. Instead, it wrapped around the prop and killed the engine. Whispering Spirit's bow was now swinging around and headed dangerously close to the shore. Frantic, she called the Harbor Master for help. It was amazing how quickly they responded. Two guys came out in their inflatable and tied a line to the bow. Then the guy wearing a wetsuit jumped in the water and cut the mooring wand line. It was Thanksgiving weekend and the water was bitterly cold. Whispering Spirit was then towed over to a new location where she was safely tethered to another mooring wand. Talk about humiliation and disgrace! Catherine sat in the cockpit stunned wondering what to do next. She was going to have to dive over the side and clear the prop of any residual line. And she didn't have a wet suit.

While mournfully taking in her pathetic plight, she looked over at a boat moored next to her and saw a guy calmly sitting in his cockpit enjoying a cup of coffee and reading a book. Catherine laughed aloud nonsensically from all her pent up emotion. Here was a guy sitting in his own bucking bronco absorbed in the pleasure of reading a book.

How she wished she could calm her own inner storms like the people in these two stories. She had much to learn about God's control over all circumstances. If she had acknowledged that Jesus was in the storm with her, would she have responded differently? Would she be able handle tense situations differently in the future?

The guy sitting peacefully in his boat next to her was curious about why she was laughing so hard and yelled over to her through the wind to ask if he could come over for a visit. He wanted to hear

Catherine's story and find out why she had just been towed. As he was rowing over in his dinghy through the chop, she noticed that he was quite handsome, and he wasn't wearing that tell-tale band of gold on his left hand. She quickly dashed below decks and did what she could to fix her hair and add some lipstick. Her kind new friend, smartly equipped with a wetsuit stowed aboard his boat, offered to come back and completely unravel the line still clinging to the prop. It turned out that they were both unattached single-handlers. Fred started calling her his *damsel in distress*, which was irritating, but not too much. They ended up embracing life together for a short period of time. It was a bitter sweet companionship. They remained friends though and Catherine visited him years later after he had moved to Mexico.

Catherine got Whispering Spirit settled on a single hook in La Paz. Even in a crowded anchorage it was better to swing on a single hook. That way all the boats could swing together in the same direction with the shifting of the currents. One boater (wouldn't you know it – a stink potter), put out a bow *and* a stern hook. After a polite discussion where he saw the reasoning behind the logic of swinging on a single hook, he brought in his stern line. *A stink potter is an impolite euphemism for a power boater because of the stinky exhaust, unlike the purity of a sailboat that is driven only by the wind (well, for the purists anyway – you know… the ones with the halos). Sailors and power boaters have an ongoing banter between them that is mostly friendly, kind of like the ongoing rivalry between UCLA and USC fans.*

Darn it. There weren't any showers for the tourists on the beach in La Paz. She had been hoping for a fresh water shower, even if it meant getting one in the great outdoors on a public beach. She used up the water in the tank for a shower in the cockpit from the hose that had been rigged up for this purpose and then went into town to do some exploring. But her first priority had to be to fill up a couple of water jugs and get them in the tanks back onboard before a second trip in just for pleasure. This temporary supply would last until she worked her way over to the dock to fill the tanks. After some exploring she treated herself to a delicious Chinese dinner at the recommendation of a store keeper. It was lovely listening to the local guitar player strumming soft Latin music in this restaurant that was quite crowded.

The next morning Catherine woke up to drizzles and surprisingly cooler temperatures. She never would have imagined it could be so chilly in Mexico. Darn it again. She had so much to do in town and now would have to slug around in wet weather. And to add to her gloomy attitude, for the first time since being in Mexican waters, she had a case of the *turistas* – must have been the Chinese food. She changed her mind about going ashore and just stayed miserably below decks to wait for everything to pass (*ho ho*).

The following morning she felt almost back to normal. The weather had cleared up too so she planned her day in town. The first stop was to pay a visit to the fish taco stand that a tourist told her she simply had to try. Oh my. Those had to be one of the greatest gifts Mexico had to offer. Never had she tasted anything so delicious. The man selling the fish tacos from his push cart that he parked in front of the pier every day was such a gentle soul. He used the freshest of ingredients and her mouth watered every time she thought of having just one more taco before dragging herself away with a happy tummy.

Fortified, it was time for the usual routine in another Mexican city of any size; i.e., laundry, shopping, propane, water, get fishing license renewed, visit Port Captain, etc. She really did need to do better with her Spanish. She found a hardware store where she was certain she could buy a plunger for the head. The only problem was that she didn't know how to say plunger in Spanish and couldn't find it in her Spanish English Dictionary. With gestures and a lame attempt to say that she wanted a *pumpa para bano* (pump for the bathroom), the store clerk politely repressed his giggles and gave directions in Spanish for where she might be able to find this item that he supposedly didn't carry. One of the things Catherine was learning about store clerks in this culture was that they know how to give you lengthy directions for what might simply be a way to get you far away from ever finding your way back into their store again. Very clever of them! Of course she got hopelessly lost but finally managed to find her way back to Whispering Spirit, her floating home sweet home. Later that afternoon she rowed the dinghy over to uninteresting-looking Mogote Island. She wanted to see if she could find any shells for her growing collection. Not much there; but it had to be explored anyway, just because.

Another memory of one of Catherine's foibles with the Spanish language was back in Ensenada in a cute little *tienda* (store) admiring some scarves that were on sale. She was surprised at how inexpensive they were and told the sales woman that they were *muy boracho*. What she meant to say was *muy barato*. The words sound so much alike. But instead of using the word for cheap, Catherine told her the scarf was drunk. No doubt the polite sales lady was laughing inside at yet another crazy *gringa* (white English-speaking female) crossing the border into her domain, but she just nodded her head. She was so gracious.

Being true to her inner nature, Catherine had quite enough of *the big city* after a week, so it was time to move on. She loved the clear waters of the Sea of Cortez. But you have to be away from a city to enjoy this luxury. The anchorages off a popular tourist spot can be quite unhealthy from boaters dumping their heads into the once pristine waters. If she couldn't go snorkeling or frolicking in the delicious warmth of clear water, she got pretty cranky. She needed the city but she was much more content in quiet anchorages far removed from the hustle and bustle and noise of populated areas.

Catherine felt closer to Jesus when she reflected on that part of her personality. He needed to escape the crowds on a regular basis to pray and get replenished before going back out into the crowds. This coming and going was Catherine's overly simplified interpretation of theology. Come and Go. That's her take on the Bible in a nutshell. Beckoning, Jesus said "Come, follow me" (Mark 1:17). Then he instructed "Therefore go and make disciples of all nations, baptizing them in the name of the Father and of the Son and of the Holy Spirit" (Matthew 28:19). So she would go to the city for provisioning and to be in community and then she returned to Jesus for his love and sustenance. Someday she hoped to learn how to make disciples. Is sharing with others the love you have for Jesus enough? She felt so inadequate in this area.

Meditative Prayer

Dear Jesus... you offer us your peace. Truly happiness flows from such a generous offer.

Journal Prompt

What will be the commerce of heaven? What medium will be used to express value? Will the exchange of ideas be worth their weight in gold? Will an act of kindness fill our bellies? Will communities nourish in creative new ways as a vehicle of fiscal responsibility tendering care for currency?

Chapter 13

SHRIMPERS

Catherine simply had to visit Pichilingue because the name was so much fun to pronounce and also because she wanted to see what this particular hurricane hole had to offer in the way of protection. As it turned out, it might be a safe place to stay in a hurricane but she wasn't very impressed. However, she did have a great experience visiting a shrimper. The fishermen aboard this vessel agreed to barter for some shrimp. She gave them a bottle of wine and a small bottle of rum. It was interesting for Catherine to get the hang of this kind of financial bartering. They filled her bucket with shrimp and she felt the price was fair. Back aboard Whispering Spirit she began the arduous task of cleaning her little prizes. It took hours to shell and devein all of them. Most were easy to devein and simply used toothpicks to pull out the blue vein on the backside of the shrimp. But then there were some that either had roe in them, or a sand vein, and she was completely grossed out. It felt like changing a poopy diaper cleaning these particular shrimp. They cooked very quickly in a large pot of boiling water. She froze about two thirds of them and settled in for enjoying a feast with the rest. She was a fan of horse radish and used this as a dipping sauce. What a delicious meal!

Probably the most unpleasant of her experiences had to do with one of God's tiniest of creatures. Not only are they tiny but they are nearly translucent. Someone told her they are called siphonophores. You can only see them while wearing a snorkeling mask in the water. Then, when you are fully immersed in the water, you can feel them.

Boy can you feel them. They are jelly fish and their sting is nasty. They seemed to come and go in various places during the hottest months, the exact time of year when you want to be in the water frequently to cool off. You don't really cool off though because the water temperature is as warm as the air temperature. But at least you can wash away sweat and grime. She wondered how shrimp and jelly fish got along. If you were to enlarge a siphonophore you would see that it has some of the physical characteristics of shrimp. Catherine couldn't help but wonder why God made creatures that are so unfriendly toward the children he lovingly created.

Meditative Prayer

How many of us could live without a television or a computer? What kind of freedom would that offer? How much time could instead be spent in communion with you dear Lord? Can you teach those of us who are comfortable with silence, to make friends with silence and appreciate the bliss of freedom from noise?

Journal Prompt

Where do you go for safety?

Chapter 14

FLYING ANGELS

While sailing in a bare whisper of wind from Pichilingue toward Isla Danzante, Catherine saw the most fascinating sight she had ever seen. Just off the bow of Whispering Spirit swam a school of large manta rays. There must have been thirty of them flying gracefully together through a glassy sea with wings like angels beckoning her to follow. Were these messengers sent by God to guide her along the way? She felt safe with them. The Bible talks about God's army made up of the heavenly host. With this army leading her in a watery charge she felt God's protection. Again God used his creatures to open Catherine's eyes. It was just like when Elisha prayed for his servant and he looked and saw the hills full of horses and chariots of fire all around them (2 Kings 6:17). How can you be with all your children at the same time Lord? Someday you will explain and it will become abundantly clear. Catherine could hardly wait.

The wind eventually picked up and she sailed at hull speed to Isla Danzante where she anchored in a narrow inlet and had the place all to herself. It was wonderful. She knew she would be able to keep the place all to herself because the inlet was too narrow for more than one boat to be anchored at a time. She backed into it cautiously and dropped both a stern and bow anchor in order to stay put and then went snorkeling and saw an eel for the first time since being in Mexican waters. She had to admit it frightened her and cut her exploring expedition short. It looked to be about five feet long and was free swimming. She made it a habit to never venture too far away when swimming and snorkeling from the place of security, whether it was Whispering Spirit, the dinghy, or land. Serpents are such nasty looking creatures and can easily inflict harm should they so desire.

The very first time she ever saw an eel was while vacationing in Hawaii. Catherine had never snorkeled before and her now ex-husband was trying to teach her. Hanauma Bay is an ideal location for snorkeling. She donned the flippers and walked backwards into the water. Then she put on the mask and snorkel. When she was waste deep he instructed her to put her head in the water and breathe naturally. Well, she put her head in the water, but she immediately began to panic. This was not something that came naturally. It took a few more attempts before she mastered her fear and was ready to float around and look at this new world of life below the ocean's surface. What she didn't like about Hanauma were the many reefs just under the waterline. She didn't trust what might be lurking in the crevices. If it was up to her she'd much rather snorkel in more open spaces. But all the interesting fish are in the reef. Snorkeling within an arm's reach of the coral meant you could easily scrape yourself on the reef. Because of the microorganisms that make up these reefs, those kinds of scrapes can take a long time to heal. Without a warning she spotted an eel and panicked. Catherine began ruffling up the water as she attempted to swim backwards to get away from it. Her husband was a pro and grabbed her hand sternly and yelled at her to calm down and just swim over it. She was such a mixture of bravado and big chicken. She didn't like the part of her that freaks out easily and wished she could be brave all the time. But if Jesus can sweat blood, then she was in good company.

Some sailors that she met in Mexico shared with her a story about their snorkeling expedition. They used a Hawaiian rubberized sling gun for catching lobster. Apparently eels take personal ownership of lobsters hidden in rock crevices. One man saw a lobster hiding in a crevice and aimed his sling. He missed the lobster and hit an eel instead. Understandably that angered the eel and it came charging at him. Lucky for the snorkelers he managed to hit the eel close to its head so he could keep it from biting him.

Catherine had an opportunity to vacation in Tahiti. While there she also spent a couple of days on the island of Bora Bora. A guide took some of the tourists out for a snorkeling trip. It was there that she had a face-to-face encounter with a shark that she guessed was also about five feet long. The guide got a good laugh at the wide-eyed look in Catherine's eyes behind the snorkeling mask as she quickly surfaced for help. Apparently that shark was like a pet to him and he took sick, sick, sick pleasure in scaring his guests half to death. Shame on him!

And speaking of nasty creatures, she was finally getting somewhat accustomed to mud daubers as companions. These wasps were never aggressive with her personally. But they were single mindedly determined to build mud nests throughout the cabin and often under the cover of the mainsail. When it was time to hoist the sail, about a dozen of these nests would drop on the deck after the cover was removed. She then swept them overboard before getting under way. They are quite frightening looking but were mostly just a nuisance. She'd never heard of anyone getting stung by one of these interlopers; nevertheless, they looked really menacing and she gave them their space as best she could. Between the mud daubers flying around the cabin and the siphonophores lurking hidden in the water, summers in the Sea of Cortez could be pretty uncomfortable. But the beauty of the place made up for these unpleasantries.

While sharing this story she will also share her experience with an unfriendly Puffer fish. These cute little creatures were quick to hover around the boat when there were some tasty morsels to share. She was hand feeding them some broken-up crackers from the cockpit when one of them decided her thumb looked as delicious as the crumbs. His friendly nip caused Catherine's thumb nail to turn a ghastly purple. Lesson learned. No more Mr. Nice Guy to Puffers.

Soaking up the sun's rays is really dumb. She knew that. But as a Southern California girl, she couldn't resist the warmth drenching her body. On Whispering Spirit her favorite place to sun bathe was on the foredeck. She would carry one of the cockpit cushions forward with her and take turns baking her front and then her back while trying not to fall asleep. She felt it was important to get a tan slowly because she was in the sun all the time. By gradually working up some color she was able to prevent herself from getting burned. Such was her logic anyway. It's so easy to justify doing what we want to do.

Meditative Prayer

Father God, let us never stray far from your protective gaze. While knowing that you watch over us wherever we are, let us want always to seek your face as well. We know that if we are consciously seeking you, then we are consciously doing our best to stay in your will.

Journal Prompt

What a challenge it is to live in two worlds! Our bodies are present on earth in the here and now, yet our hearts long for eternity and God's kingdom come. How do we walk in this awareness to be a blessing to others as we seek to be a blessing to God?

Chapter 15

HURRICANE HOLE

Puerto Escondido is the other reputed safe haven in the Sea of Cortez to run to for shelter from impending storms. Catherine learned from the VHF weather channel that there was a potential hurricane headed her way. A deep fear crept into her at this unwelcome news so she headed for the protection of this anchorage. It was fully enclosed by surrounding hills with a very narrow entrance. Many other boats also headed for this bay at the news. We all anchored on multiple hooks with plenty of scope, or so she thought. Just as the wind was seriously starting to pick up, in came the local shrimpers. To Catherine, these are gorgeous boats even if scarred and battered. There is a delicacy about them in their heartiness with all the booms and lines trailing the water starboard, port, and aft. From a distance one could imagine them looking like a Dutch hat. But the fishermen were either callous or foolishly confident of their anchoring techniques in a storm. They dropped only a single hook with hardly any scope and then went ashore presumably to their lodgings.

No hurricane. The threat passed. Fear, along with the wind, had a chance to slowly dissipate. Isn't this true of most fears? The shrimpers went back out to sea and the yachties hauled in all their anchors except the one bow hook. Life went back to some sense of normalcy.

The most excitement we experienced after the scare of a hurricane was spotting a pilot whale that had found its way into the bay. Do whales need protection from storms too? Catherine couldn't imagine why it went in there but it was beautiful to watch. She only hoped it made its way out of the bay safely.

There was sweetness to the days in this place. The boaters awoke to the sound of bells. A herd of goats made their way along the hillside trail very early every day and then back again as the sun was setting. They were a reminder that she was living in a foreign country, or at least in an environment foreign to her since she'd never lived where goats were prevalent. In Old Testament times a goat was used as a sin offering where the priest had "to lay both hands on the head of the live goat and confess over it all the wickedness and rebellion of the Israelites-all their sins-and put them on the goat's head" (Leviticus 16:21). In these days of the new covenant all our sins for all time were placed on the head of one man. It's strange to think of Jesus as a scapegoat. But thanks to his sacrifice, atonement with God is something we can claim for ourselves. Jesus opened the door to salvation and made it so incredibly easy for us to enter through. He sacrificed his life on a cross to cleanse us from our sins. For all who seek him he "stand[s] at the door and knock[s]. If anyone hears [his] voice and opens the door, [he] will come in..." (Revelation 3:20). He couldn't possibly have made it any easier for us. Catherine wholeheartedly opened the door. Now she wants to learn about this God who says "I have called you friends..." (John 15:15).

It was in this delightful community of boaters that Catherine learned how to bake bread. She didn't know who began the lovely tradition, but she was given some sour dough starter by one of the cruising ladies who shared some of her precious gift. The bread rose throughout the day while sitting on top of the cabin under the warmth of the sun. The smell was intoxicating.

On shore there was a little *tienda* where the owner sold all kinds of things from canned goods to fishing tackle to hardware. He owned a small parrot that he kept in a cage just outside the store. Catherine loved to visit this colorful little winged creature. She did wonder if it was unhappy at not being allowed to fly freely. We are so used to seeing parakeets caged, but little parrots? Don't they belong in the wild? Does one's personality change when kept under lock and key? Does the soul ever adapt to being controlled in a limiting environment? Do we ever learn we are free to be unique? Some do. She wondered if she was learning. Is it a matter of giving someone permission to control us? Sometimes bondage is self-imposed. Sometimes divorce is necessary. Sometimes we need to find a different job or different friends. But sometimes, like Paul, we need to just deal with our thorns and let grace be sufficient (2 Corinthians 12:7-9) and find peace in any situation.

Catherine couldn't remember why, but a boating couple gave her a gift of a Pothos plant they had named Hèja, which means hawk in Hungarian. It never flew away. Hèja and several members of its offspring are still alive and thriving with Catherine today. Maybe freedom is only a fanciful dream. Maybe some of us don't really want true freedom. Maybe there's too much responsibility involved in being in charge of one's own destiny. Or maybe some of us do want freedom, only within the boundaries of God's directives and guidance.

While even this lovely secluded anchorage could get too crowded, she did manage to find a secret spot and took off for an hour or two of total privacy almost every afternoon. Rowing the Avon inflatable was great exercise. Her secluded spot was around the corner from the main open area. There was a large rock in the center. First she placed the oars, snorkel, and mask securely on a ledge of the rock, then got in the water and flipped the dinghy over. The rubber of the dinghy can get scalding hot, so she first had to make sure she splashed some water in the middle before hopping back on board. Lying in that pool of warm water under the sun was a touch of paradise. And it was so very quiet.

How should we think of Jesus, our truest beloved, as a lover? We are flesh, as he created us, and he came in the flesh. Man and woman are sexual beings. Yet even passages from the Song of Solomon are too sensual for readings at weddings. Catherine knew this first hand. She had been a wedding coordinator for a few years and had to let the prospective bridal couples know that they were not permitted to select Scripture from the beautiful Song of Songs. The imagery wasn't appropriate for sharing at a holy ceremony according to the guidelines of the church.

How should we love you Jesus? Our visual image of you is too human. She found it almost easier to love God the Father because she had no physical image of him. This is of course true of Holy Spirit as well. Yet with deep reverence and awe she quoted Gabriel's response to Mary's pondering with "The Holy Spirit will come on you, and the power of the Most High will overshadow you" (Luke 1:35). Here's a poem about this amazing conversation.

Each member of the Trinity loves us individually, wholly, and holy with an almost unspeakable love that is so difficult to grasp. But Catherine was learning much about this love on her quest through the heavenly and physical components of life aboard a small sailboat in foreign waters.

She knew she was a failure at marriage. There was a drastic age difference in both her marriages and she was very young. Looking back she saw them as men who would take care of her. She wasn't proud of that part of her personality. Her independent nature came later. One husband expected perfection, something she was unable to give him – who could? She tried very hard to be all that he wanted her to be which is probably where she first developed her not-good-enough persona. Because she worked so hard at trying to be good enough, she developed abilities that led to her being independent, perhaps too independent. And that holds another kind of sadness. Wounds take such a long time to heal. She had to be honest and say that she was relieved to be out of the marriages. Repenting assuaged her guilt and prepared her for allowing the healing to begin… "Then young women will dance and be glad, young men and old as well. I will turn their mourning into gladness; I will give them comfort and joy instead of sorrow" (Jeremiah 31:13).

There were times when Catherine thought she'd like to take the plunge again. She believed age was not a prohibitor to a desire to love and be loved. Jesus was teaching her how to love him. Yet she struggled to know how to keep him at the center of her love while allowing another to enter her realm of deep longing? This was a

A Protestant's Adoration

Her burden of love was uniquely designed

far greater than she could have imagined.

Hers was a missive personally signed.

Gabriel spoke and she listened.

A humble maiden chosen by God,

overtaken in wonder, overshadowed by love.

In rhythm with time this journey she trod

harboring hope from the promise above.

In hour appointed, a hush filled the night.

This secret once held by a woman so fair

still rings out its message of heaven's delight

yet offered in Blessing to those in despair.

You gave of your Son, as did God, for me.

I offer you my love most tenderly.

mystery to her. She wanted to share Jesus' love on an intimate level with another who was also lost and found in the eyes of our savior. Perhaps time and drawing ever nearer to her Lord would one day bring resolution from what seems like such an unsolvable conflict.

If she were married and had a child, and that child was about to be married to a wonderful partner, she would be happy for them both. Maybe that's how she should think of God's love. She was his child. He wanted her to be happy. It makes him happy when she is happy. God would not be jealous of someone she chose to marry and would bless a union with another believer. She would not be forsaking her love for God when she entered holy matrimony. Our family would just be a little larger.

Catherine needed to cool off and slid into the water swimming naturally with the fish in their coverings of skin and scales. When her body temperature returned back to normal, she donned the snorkel and mask. What an amazing world there is just below the surface of the water. With her mask on she could see so much of what was hidden and she was instantly united in kinship with God's other creatures. One of her favorite species of fish is called a Trumpet Fish. It appears to be about three feet long, is skinny, and its snout looks just like a trumpet. They are adorable and come in many beautiful colors. She saw a tiny Sculpin. Since their sting is venomous, she gave it plenty of leeway. Then all of a sudden a plume of indigo burst in front of her. She had frightened a tiny octopus and it had spewed out its warning. When the ink cleared she marveled at such an adorable creature. She would love to have held it and feel its arms entangling her hand. She swam on and was startled by yet another creature. Maybe she should clarify that they startled each other. A ray was snuggled in its hiding place beneath the sand until Catherine got too close. In an instant it flew out leaving a sand cloud in its wake.

Meeting Jesus was like the times she was startled by the octopus and the ray. He often came upon her at times when she thought her fortifications of emotion were under control. She had memories of him doing this to her in church. She'd be sitting peacefully and attentively listening to a sermon by the most endearing of pastors when she would get caught off guard and tears would begin streaming down her face. It happens in an instant. Sometimes she would let the tears take their course and flow freely in humble adoration, especially when the church lights were dimmed for worship. In moments like those she wondered why she had any doubts at all. She couldn't understand why she needed constant reminders of his love? Snorkeling presents the challenge of a fogged-up mask when she got all emotionally charged over God's explosions of creation. In church she could grab a Kleenex to mop up the tears. While snorkeling she had to pause and use some spit to un-fog her mask so she could see clearly again. A Scripture passage came to mind, "He took the blind man by the hand and led him outside the village. When he had spit on the man's eyes and put his hands on him, Jesus asked, 'Do you see anything?'" (Mark 8:23).

Yes Jesus, Catherine saw you. She loved how Jesus cleared up what seems blurry until we are ready for more revelations. In his perfect timing he lifts the veil little by little when he knows we're ready to take understanding to a higher level.

Meditative Prayer

Dear Heavenly Father. We know it is your will that we be in community with believers. But in church, is it terrible to want to worship alone while in community? Is that wrong? For single people, sometimes our expression of adoration is more sincere when we don't personally know the person sitting on our side. When we're alone in community, our focus is on you as we look upward. Yet we can be comforted by the great crowd of witnesses surrounding us. Our love for you is personal, yet also corporate. When we raise our hands, they elevate to you alone my King. Such is the blessing of being single. We have a direct line of communication.

Journal Prompt

What does our relationship with God look like when we are alone with him, when we are with our brothers and sisters in a community group, and when we are in a church service? We can perhaps relate by envisioning Jesus alone with his Father and Holy Spirit hovering, with his disciples and closest friends, and with the vast crowds of seekers.

Chapter 16

CLAMS

The furthest north Catherine went into the Sea of Cortez was to Bahia de Concepcion. It is a very long inlet and without any hesitation she could say that it was her absolute favorite port of call. The water was so clear it was as if there wasn't any water at all. What made that place so unique was the ease of getting clams. There was an abundant supply and all she had to do was swim to a place where the water was about six feet deep, then by swishing her flippers back and forth, she revealed the clams that were sitting just below the sand's surface. She then just reached down and picked up a handful and added them to the netted bag with the cinched closure. There were several different varieties of clams. She found out one species was called chocolates (sounds more interesting pronounced with a Spanish accent; kind of like *chock o lattes*). They were delicious when steamed and dipped in lemon juice.

She lingered for about a week doing various chores like polishing the stainless, oiling the teak, scrubbing the keel and the hull, cleaning the lifelines, and removing debris from the anchor chain. She wanted to get the boat in great condition before heading over to the mainland of Mexico where the water wouldn't be so clear. It rains more often on the Pacific side of Mexico and Central America and that causes a lot of mud and silt to run into the water making it murky.

Part of a poem she wrote about this place was her attempt to capture how alluring Jesus, her true Captain, the ultimate fisherman, was to her. If he were to take her home during any part of this journey, she would have wanted it to be here.

Concepcion

Concepcion with your waters crystal blue

I could swim and float forever so enraptured by your warmth.

Is it my Pisces nature that draws me nigh to thee?

Or is it this fisherman's net that's captured me?

I swam among the fishes until the Captain took me home.

Entangled in your beauty, living water, I am yours.

For the Lamb at the center of the throne will be their shepherd;

he will lead them to springs of living water.

And God will wipe away every tear from their eyes.

Revelation 7:17

Meditative Prayer

How easy it is to pray to you Lord! You have given us such a variety of ways to communicate with you. We can talk to you as if to another person in the room. We can write love letters to you in a journal. We can sing songs of praise to you in worship. We can recite the Our Father. We can create prayers from Psalms. How wonderful it is to have so many, many ways to express our thoughts to you.

Journal Prompt

How can we stop making prayer problematic?

Chapter 17

TRINITY

Trying to understand the Trinity is challenging. Catherine wondered if she could think of God, in some small way, like a marriage united in love. Most married couples are joined with the same last name on their wedding day. Once the vows are taken the Pastor introduces the couple for the first time as Mr. and Mrs. Smith. They each still have their own unique first names, but now they have the same last name. With God as a viable witness to wedding vows, a marriage is a triune relationship of sorts. Husband and wife become joined together with God. She hoped the Lord would forgive her for this very poor analogy to try and understand him. He is God the Father, God the Son, and God the Holy Spirit united as one.

She thought of how often she'd been out for a walk and watched an elderly couple heading toward her on their stroll in the park. They looked as though they had been happily married for many years as they held hands and looked adoringly into each other's eyes. They knew each other so well that they were almost as one. Jesus said, "I and the Father are one" (John 10:30).

Catherine was well aware that she won't know the fullness of the Trinity until she's brought home to his Kingdom yet to come. In the meantime God provided her enough for the moment to understand him. And since he is God she didn't expect to understand fully – yet. It seemed to her that God is a God who constantly asks his people to be patient and wait upon him. His people of the former covenant waited expectantly for the Messiah and there are many Scriptures that reflect this hope. His people of the new covenant now wait expectantly for Christ's return. Waiting with expectancy means that we have to trust in the fulfillment of what has been promised. There's so much Catherine didn't understand. What does she do when in the middle of a seemingly impossible mess? God asks us time and again not to be afraid. Then why, she wondered, was she afraid so often? She has witnessed God take her out of all kinds of troubles. She needed to trust that he would get her out of future messes. She needed to learn to "trust in the Lord with all [her] heart and lean not on [her] own understanding" (Proverbs 3:5). It's easy to quote Scripture. It's ever so hard to live through God's promises, especially when we're in the middle of the fire. If there are only two choices – to believe, or not believe – then why wouldn't we all choose to believe? I'm trying Lord, Catherine pleaded. She knew her faith was growing. She begged that God would please be patient with her in her many weaknesses.

Meditative Prayer

Will we ever be satisfied with our level of faith? Are you Lord? If you are, it's not clear why you should be. Maybe that's why this story is called Sailing Toward Faith. Faith is a Journey, isn't it? You are our destination. And the way to you is through faith. This is actually quite a wonderful journey – seeking you always and everywhere. Give us the strength we need to continue the journey because sometimes we are so sad not seeing you face to face.

Journal Prompt

A loving father is patient with his children. What does it mean to you to hear the Psalmist say that God's rod and staff bring comfort to him?

Chapter 18

RETRACING FOOTSTEPS

As Catherine retraced some of the routes she'd taken so far in order to return to Los Frailles where she would cross over to the mainland of Mexico, she stopped off at Isla Partida near La Paz. Since Whispering Spirit seemed to be the only boat anchored off the island, and she believed the island to be uninhabited, she decided it would be a good place to practice using her shot gun. She brought several paper plates with her to set up as targets. She attached a paper plate to a scrub brush so it would be upright as she practiced her shooting. She felt like she did ok. But her shoulder hurt for several days and her ear had ringing in it for just about as long. Catherine felt safer having a shotgun aboard than if she had no protection at all. She only hoped she would never, ever, feel compelled to use it or, God forbid, have it used against her.

Her true weapon of choice was her trusty Sword – the Word of God, and prayer. She was gaining faith in this armor of protection. Holy Spirit would guide her as she learned to trust her advocate and counselor. In teenage years she was open to false teachings and tried meditating on some single word in order to clear her mind and find God. That might work for some. She was just not sure it was the best way to have a relationship with Jesus. First of all, clearing her mind was impossible. More importantly, she never saw anything in the Bible that instructed her to do this. If Jesus didn't practice repetitive word mantras, then she believed he had no desire for us to do it either. Jesus simply talked to his Father in normal communication like she talked to her friends, or Sophia.

She wondered about intercessory prayer. Isn't God capable of interceding for us without prayer? Maybe prayer is God's way of encouraging us to care for each other to get our minds off of ourselves. But history teaches us about prayer that is powerful enough to even change the plans of God. Prayer is relationship. It is relating with God. God is with us always, but we are not always consciously with God. Prayer consciously places us in his holy presence. It changes us. Prayer reminds us that we are not in control. It is up to God as to whether or not he wants to change his mind through our prayers. We may cry out fervently to God, but we have no right to make demands, only pleas. She should clarify. She was not comfortable making demands of God.

Growing up spiritually can and should be simple. Catherine didn't know why she always needed to make things so difficult. By letting go of contemplative practices she also felt a need to mourn the loss of her innocence. She had to face the fact that Satan is alive and doing his best to interrupt her relationship with God. She was beginning to see how Satan was oozing his way into people's lives, like an erupting volcano spewing vomit over sacred ground. Jesus is the ONLY way to God and salvation and eternity. Believers must hang on to this truth and never be deceived, as "if that were possible" (Matthew 24:24).

She was ready to make the crossing over to the next major leg of the journey. Whispering Spirit was in good shape and her larders were full. It was sad to leave the Sea of Cortez behind, but new adventures awaited her and she was ready to move on. She needed to finish the race of running away from the unknown and find rest once and for all in the loving arms of Jesus. Once she could accept that Jesus was everywhere, it wouldn't matter where she was. It's the running away that's wrong. She needed to find out how to be still and present wherever she was. Goals are good things. But goals that don't include joy in the moment defeat life's purpose because of never fully accepting who we are right now.

Meditative Prayer

How is it possible to be taught about you as a child, but that knowledge didn't grow? Why didn't it stick? Yet frequently many of us had our hearts pound at your name. For many of us it takes years before something happens and we finally let you in. Help us to repent for it taking so long. Help us to repent with both sadness and great joy. Thank you for never giving up on us, even in our darkest hours. Freedom awakens our senses to, thankfully, never wanting to retrace our steps or regress into our sinful past. We praise you Lord Jesus.

Journal Prompt

Do you remember your former self? Or are you still living a life without Jesus Christ the Messiah? Take the gift. He loves you so much. You don't have to understand. None of us fully comprehend, yet. But look at the historical realities of his life. Let all his many miracles speak for themselves that Jesus is God. Begin the journey of repentance and salvation. It's the most important thing you will ever do. Allow yourself to trust. Read the Bible. Go to church. Be with believers. Get baptized. Take communion. Let someone pray with you and for you. Be blessed.

Chapter 19

SO MANY BIRDS

The crossing was thankfully uneventful. As Catherine approached Isla Isabella the first thing she saw from a fair distance away was a halo of birds swarming the island. She'd never seen anything like it before. There were literally hundreds of birds flying over this little island. It was like she was entering another era in time. She was almost afraid to disembark Whispering Spirit and row the dinghy ashore. What if she were landing in the Garden of Eden? If she were, would she ever care about returning to the real world?

What a variety of birds! Tropicbirds are white with very long tails and they swarmed Isla Isabella like hovering angels. While exploring, Catherine came upon shrubs that were exploding with color from Frigate Birds in the middle of their courtship. The males have red pouches that inflate like balloons to attract the females. Apparently she got a little too close to the action and one by one the pouches deflated. Oops – sorry guys. She left and gave them back their privacy. A little further on in her hike she came across nesting Blue-footed boobies with their chicks. She was certain she had never seen anything so astonishingly endearing in her whole life. These birds have honest-to-goodness sky-blue feet. The chicks were all fluffy white. There were also egrets and pelicans everywhere. She expected God to appear at any moment strolling happily in his garden.

She must have been in a daze because when she got back to the dinghy she began dragging it to the water's edge before untying it from the tree trunk. Some locals on the beach had just given her some of their freshly-caught fish. They got a good laugh as the crazy gringa came to a screeching halt at the end of the tether. But they doubled over in hysteria when she flipped the Avon while rowing out through the surf losing all the contents of the dinghy, not to mention her pride. She wondered if God was snickering at his crazy kid too. Such is life. At least then she didn't feel so guilty about not paying for the fish. They got their payment in a good laugh at her expense. But as a friend of hers often said... it's all good.

Meditative Prayer

Why do we carry the heavy burden of fear so often? The Bible tells us not to fear. Yet we do. And how often does our fear prove itself to have been a lie, a waste of precious energy, a needless loss of sleep? Please dear Heavenly Father, help us to rest in you. Help us to be obedient to your son's command that we not toil in fear. Guide us Holy Spirit to trust.

Journal Prompt

Let us remind ourselves of every fear that was needless. Let us learn to laugh at ourselves and lean more on Christ.

Chapter 20

DEMONS AND SEA SNAKES

Is there evil in the world? You bet there is. Catherine had seen so much of it that her heart had been tested to the point of being nearly irrevocably shattered. Her heart was completely torn apart one day in class. This was not the kind of heartache that comes from a relationship betrayal. This was heartache of a God-sized proportion. In graduate school she chose for her thesis a topic about modern-day slavery.

Catherine saw herself as a gentle soul, so why she chose such a horrific thesis was baffling to her. Maybe she wanted to get out of her own pity party of hurts that continued to cast such a deep gloom within her. But one day in class she met God in an epiphany that continually percolates within her. Just when she thought she'd learned about all the evils she could possibly stomach, she was about to face yet another one even more horrid than the others. Three of her classmates enacted out a play about witchcraft. The plot had to do with the plight of an uneducated Caribbean woman who lived in poverty. Her baby was sick. She went to a witch doctor to see if he knew of a cure. For a hefty sum he convinced her that the only way to cure this kind of illness was to pour boiling water over the baby.

That's when Catherine ran from the room. There was an empty classroom across the hall and she stood by the window sobbing convulsively. It was winter and the weather was unusually cold. There were trees in the distance. It was still early in the morning. The fog was dissipating and rays of sparkling sunshine were shining through the tree tops. On the outside of the window in front of her were drops of melting frost. She was crying so hard that she could not distinguish her tears from the drops slithering down the window pane. She laid her burning forehead against the coolness of the glass for comfort. Somehow she knew in that moment that God was crying with her. He also abhors the pain of his children. She wasn't alone in her distress. She had a God who knows pain and suffering. While she was crying, she remembered that "Jesus wept" (John 11:35).

Isla Isabella disappeared slowly behind her. She was about to enter the Bay of Banderas heading toward Puerto Vallarta. Her first stop was to anchor just around Punta de Mita so she could get cleaned up before entering the harbor. Here was where she again met evil face to face. She saw her very first sea snake. It was swimming along the surface of the water. She heard that if you get bitten by a sea snake you will die quickly. Thankfully their mouths are very small and can't open very wide, so they can only bite areas like the skin between your fingers. This knowledge didn't exactly offer much in the way of comfort. So she was torn. Should she risk jumping over the side for a quick bath, or forfeit this luxury for the sake of safety? She decided to chance it. After surveying the water around Whispering Spirit, she jumped into the ocean to get wet and climbed up the swim ladder as quickly as she could. She lathered up. After another careful scan of the water she jumped back in to rinse off, again getting out of the water as fast as she possibly could. With that chore behind her she set sail for the marina in Puerto Vallarta. She counted a total of twenty six sea snakes slithering menacingly about on the surface of the water. She felt somewhat guilty referring to them as evil. Sea snakes and humans are simply natural enemies. Their ability to poison their victims leading to death is their protection. Is that why people inject poison in the lives of others? Are we attempting to protect ourselves when we intentionally, or unintentionally, hurt people? She needed to reconsider the meaning of evil. It would be awhile before she worked up her courage to swim again. For the next month or so almost all of her clean-up efforts would be on terra firma.

A Pastor and his wife taught Catherine some lessons about trust. She was a complete stranger to them and yet they began a friendship with her that she cherished. She was reminded of the Scripture "Do not let your hearts be troubled" (John 14:1). She loves what the NIV notes for this passage proclaim, "The apostles had just received disturbing news. Trust. The antidote for a troubled heart." Catherine had so much to learn about trust. Meeting people who had proven to her that they were trustworthy was a huge step toward healing. When she met this Pastor for the first time he was teaching about the broken heart at a friend's home where she was an invited guest.

She couldn't help but compare the sinister countenance of the sea snakes to the evils she had encountered in life. Most of us learn about the devil portrayed as a serpent in the Garden of Eden. We then learn about the devil as he plays havoc in our lives in sinister ways causing us to have one broken heart after another. Whispering Spirit was my sailing vessel. We are also vessels. Each time our heart is broken our vessel cracks a little allowing some joy to escape. Jesus is the antidote for our broken hearts. He knows about a broken heart. He died of one. Yes, he knows about my broken heart. When he rose from the dead he opened the door to healing. But unless we give all our pain to the only one who can heal us, any blessing he has to offer will leak out of our broken vessel. Catherine gave her heart to Jesus. Her journey toward trust had begun. She finally allowed Jesus to see her and learned how to let go of old demons so he could fight her battles for her. She spent several days pondering all the evil things that tortured her broken heart and began giving them one by one to the only one who could save her and heal her. Once she repented of sins she'd committed they no longer existed. Poof – they were gone. Like magic, she never had to worry about them again. Satan can no longer harass her with old sins because they don't exist any longer. Catherine loved how this dear Pastor reminded her of how Jesus gives us his peace. In order to not have peace, she would need to give it away. Therefore, we need to hold on tightly to the peace that Jesus gives.

Meditative Prayer

Dear Lord: How do we get to that internal space where you are all the approval we need? How do we finally overcome our insane feeling that we're never good enough? How can we learn to live in community without needing anyone's approval? What is our purpose? What can we contribute that is uniquely us before we get to be with you in that mysterious place referred to as eternity? What if you won't let us come home until we've accomplished that which you set out for us to do? How do we get past the many failures and humiliations to reach that heavenly finish line? And how will we know when we've reached the goal of that which you've directed us to do? And then what do we do about the ever-lurking what's next?

Journal Prompt

Holy Spirit can help us to fight evil. Is he your source for combat?

Chapter 21

TOURIST TRAP

Puerto Vallarta is probably Mexico's largest tourist trap. The mainland of Mexico is drastically different from Baja and the Sea of Cortez. Catherine wasn't sure she was going to like cruising in this vastly different landscape. She preferred the clear waters of the Sea of Cortez. The water along the mainland of the Pacific side of Mexico was going to be murky from the muddy river water flowing down from the mountains and into the ocean. She would just have to have an open mind and a determination to enjoy a different kind of beauty. She planned to make the marina of Puerto Vallarta her home for about a month. In a way she was enjoying the prospect of settling down, sort of, for a little while anyway.

After talking with some of the other yachties who had been there for a long time, she found out something that would be humorous had it not been so nerve wracking. When the cruise ships come in they use their side thrusters to snuggle up to the dock once they've entered the wide open area of the marina. This was great for them but a nightmare for the boats at anchor. Everyone knew what to do. As soon as word spread that a cruise ship was scheduled to enter the port and begin the sideways crab crawl, the boaters grabbed their whisker poles and prepared to fend off the dance that was about to begin. Whisker poles serve multiple purposes and more often than not are used for things other than simply holding the jib out when sailing downwind. The dance Catherine was referring to was like a square dance where dancers swirl around and change partners. Only the goal of the boaters was not to grab a partner, but to fend off that dancing boat that was twirling in a little too close for comfort. Some yachties seemed to think that tying fenders off the side of the boat was protection enough. How discourteous for all the rest of us who were diligently protecting the investments in their boats that are sometimes referred to as *a hole in the water that you pour money into*. After a few days of these obnoxious dances it was time to seriously consider investing in a slip inside the marina.

Another aspect of being anchored in the Puerto Vallarta marina was having the Mexican Navy based in the same port. Every morning boaters awoke to the sound of bugle revelry. Catherine got a kick out of it. Then at night they would oftentimes play another kind of music – *musica romantica*. She became quite the fan of their romantic music. But it made her burden of being single that much harder to endure.

One of the benefits of being in a slip was having access to the marina's showers. Until she had decided to rent a slip, Catherine discovered another way to get her pampering fresh-water showers. The only downside was that she had to expose herself to looking like a complete idiot. But to her a shower meant much more than mere vanity. It was a necessity to living in polite society. She gathered up shampoo, soap, and towel, put on a bathing suit, wrapped herself in a beautiful pareu, and rowed over to the dock while it was high tide. Then she walked over to the fancy hotel next door and took advantage of their outdoor showers. These were actually intended for guests of the hotel to rinse off before returning to their rooms. It was a little challenging trying to be discreet shampooing hair and cleaning privates while in the public eye. No more will be said on this. Thankfully she never got busted by the fancy hotel shower police.

Before moving into a slip she wanted to explore the city before the next cruise ship was expected to arrive in a couple of days. There's a local bus that stops at the end of the walkway where the cruise ship docks. You can ride this bus for practically nothing for the three-mile trip into town. A taxi is too costly. Catherine had a whole page of things she wanted to do in town the next day. One of the items on the checklist was having all her clothes cleaned again in fresh water at the *lavamatica*.

Morning had arrived and she was ready for her first trip to the famous town of Puerto Vallarta. It seemed abnormally hot that morning which challenged her normally good humor. She loaded up the dinghy with laundry in a netted bag and shouldered her largest backpack which was already sticking to her back with sweat. The timing of the trip was good because the tide was up. She rowed the Avon over to the now empty dock, tied it up to a piling, and climbed the rope ladder carrying her laundry the short distance to the pavement. The tide can vary up to fifteen feet so timing is everything. It was easy climbing the rope ladder with an empty backpack and dry laundry. It was only a short walk to the local bus stop and she didn't have to wait long before a very rickety-looking bus showed up. It was packed with locals and there was standing room only. She felt like a sardine squashed amongst sweaty bodies. Some of the locals had chickens with them and a couple had pigs in their laps. The worst part of the trip was hitting the cobblestoned streets. Catherine's sea legs hadn't adjusted to walking on pavement yet let alone trying to keep balance while standing on a bus bouncing on cobblestone streets.

The first stop was to find the *lavamatica* and load dirty laundry into washers. Then she had time to leisurely walk around town exploring the outdoor market, the waterfront, and some gift shops. She stopped for a *helado* (ice cream) to enjoy while walking around town. Then she found a place to have lunch where she could watch the colorful array of tourists and locals. Fortified, it was time to start loading up the backpack with groceries. With that completed she went back to the *lavamatica* to retrieve her clean, wet, and now very heavy laundry – still no dryers. The bus ride back was no better. There was still standing room only. When she finally got back to the dock, the tide was out. Catherine very carefully dropped the laundry bag into the dinghy and was absolutely ecstatic that it landed safely without falling into the water. Any shred of good humor that she had left would have vanished in an instant if all that work was for naught. When she got back onboard Whispering Spirit the first thing she had to do was put the groceries away. Then she got out the clothes pins and started hanging all the wet laundry on the lifelines, the back stay, and over the boom to dry. She had definitely earned her glass of sherry that day.

On another trip into town she visited the River Cuale. On one side of the river there were very expensive and wonderfully colored houses picturesquely lining the hillside. On the other side of the river was where poverty reigned. Watching women doing their laundry in the river held fascination for Catherine. Her appreciation for her gender went up in that moment. Women are amazing creatures. We're tough and resilient on the outside while being soft and pliable on the inside. But don't cross us, or may God help you. What must it be like for the people living on either side of the river to look out their windows and see such extreme living conditions in their neighborhood? Do the people living in the expensive homes wish the river was a wall instead of flowing water so they wouldn't have to look at the faces of poverty so close to them?

Catherine remembered a time in her life when every single day she drove past a park bench and saw a homeless woman just sitting there. One day she stopped off at a bakery and bought her breakfast. Catherine remembered feeling extremely nervous as she parked the car and approached the homeless woman. She put the food down next to her and just sat with her for a few moments in silence before getting on with her busy day. She will never forget that moment.

She remembered another similar situation when she saw a man and a woman walking the neighborhood where she worked. They were obviously homeless. She trailed behind him looking bedraggled, sad, and lost. He kept yelling at her about who knows what. She had a different pair of horribly worn out shoes on each foot. It was December. Catherine put together a bag full of clothes and excitedly looked for them the next day. When they walked by she ran after them and sheepishly handed the bag to the man. He blessed me. Every time she saw them after that they weren't wearing any of the clothes they had been given. And then she saw them no longer. There are some things in this life that Catherine was afraid she just didn't understand. This was one. Were they for real, or were they some kind of actors working their trade? Even if they were tricksters, God saw her heart. She hoped that was enough.

The day following her visit to the River Cuale she felt terribly depressed and wasn't really sure why. This cruising thing was not as glamorous as people might think. It was extremely hard work. Catherine was pretty brave, but there were a few times when she was scared out of her mind. She knew there would be more frightening times ahead of her too. She questioned, for the umpteenth time, whether or not this trip was really worth the trouble. She knew it was an adventure of a lifetime but kept thinking about being back on land and living in a sweet little home somewhere and working like normal people do. Her inheritance money wouldn't last forever and she missed hot showers. Whispering Spirit had been in her family for many years and she was showing signs of wear, just like Catherine. She missed having water come out of a tap with a seemingly endless supply. She missed seeing meat wrapped up in cellophane like it wasn't really a dead animal. The mold was beginning to get to her with its smell below decks and in her clothes. And she had no idea where she was going. She was just drifting along without a destination. Maybe she should have renamed the boat Drifter. The only real destination she had was the one in her heart. Developing a solid relationship with Father, Jesus, and Holy Spirit was her true destiny and she would sail as long as she dared to make peace with that objective. She hated it when she got whiny. So, like David, she would "Put [her] hope in God, for I will [she would] yet praise him, my [her] Savior and my [her] God" (Psalm 42:5-6).

Catherine knew what would boost her spirits. It was a gorgeous day for sailing. She took Whispering Spirit for a day trip to explore the coastline of Puerto Vallarta. She sailed past some stunning rock formations off Mismaloya Beach and saw some killer whales. Then she changed her mind about returning and instead headed for Yelapa at the southernmost part of Banderas Bay to spend the night. Was that ever a mistake! It was so rolly that she nearly got sea sick for the first time. She had to get off the boat and go ashore and just sit. After she had calmed down she joined a group of people on a hike to check out the waterfall. It was beautiful. After the hike she went back to her same beach bar spot and ordered one of those fancy drinks with a paper umbrella and wondered how she was going to survive the night. The best solution to queasiness onboard a boat is just to lie down. Somehow she did survive the night but got out of that miserable anchorage at first light. She had finally justified paying for a slip.

Her neighbor inside the marina lived aboard the most dazzling sailboat she had ever seen. It had white leather furniture in the divan and an aft sleeping compartment with a queen-sized bed and a Jacuzzi. It was definitely a party boat though and kept her up until the wee hours. There were six people aboard with a destination of Tahiti.

It was amazing just how many party animals there are cruising aboard sailboats. Catherine did join in a few times with others as they gathered for happy hour, but she was much happier being alone. She just didn't fit in with that kind of crowd. People seemed to lose their inhibitions and sense of decency while cruising. Nudity was not unusual. Seeing some guy urinate over the stern wasn't unusual either. And then there was the time she saw a guy sitting on a plastic bucket on the foredeck reading a magazine. He waved as she sailed by but Catherine was too shocked to wave back. She guessed she was just a prude of sorts because she just wanted to get away from people who lacked propriety. Local Mexicans must have thought horribly about such unseemly behavior and she felt ashamed of people in her culture that would disobey the norms of their host culture, of any culture for that matter. Living aboard a boat does not mean that you are living in a country of your own making. There are still societal norms for gracious people to abide by.

Another tourist spot she visited was Chico's Paradise where she enjoyed a delicious lunch, had a large and colorful Makah sit on her arm, and watched a spider monkey entertaining the guests by swinging in the rafters under the palapa roof. The restaurant overlooked a river and she had the joy of watching children playing on the rocks and diving into the water. While there she met a married couple who invited her to visit them in their home. They had a spectacular house overlooking the ocean. It was while visiting them that Catherine first learned about a violent squall that Mexicans call a *chubasco*. What a sight! We were enjoying lemonade on the deck when Catherine saw something in the distance that didn't look quite right. When she pointed it out to her hosts they got wide eyed and immediately went into action giving her urgent directions for what to do – fast! We gathered up the patio furniture and brought it inside and closed up all the windows. They barely got some towels down to seal off the bottom of the door when the squall of wind and rain hit. It didn't last long, but it was frighteningly powerful. She was so glad Whispering Spirit was snug in a slip. And now she had one more thing to worry about in this cruising adventure.

Another Scripture… "The wind blows wherever it pleases. You hear its sound, but you cannot tell where it comes from or where it is going. So it is with everyone born of the Spirit" (John 3:8). And "But you will receive power when the Holy Spirit comes on you" (Acts 1:8). Catherine would like to have that kind of power. Imagine having a power as strong as a *chubasco* to keep the evil one at bay. Come to me Holy Spirit Catherine prayed.

One evening while listening to the ham radio, an emergency patch came over the airways requesting help for a woman on a boat in Acapulco. She had been bitten by a bat. Someone else also listening in found help and she was flown to UCLA for rabies treatment. How frightening! A prayer was quickly said that she'd be ok. The ham radio is a true life saver for staying connected with society. There's something about hearing stories involving catastrophes in people's lives that manifests in an inner maelstrom. You realize just how short life is and begin to wonder what you are missing and what you should be doing before it becomes too late.

Catherine loved the sound of fun words. Another Mexican town that she simply had to visit was Tlaquepaque located near Guadalajara. She loved art work and Tlaquepaque was famous for being an artisan town. Because visiting Tlaquepaque (it's such a fun word to say) meant a very long drive, Catherine thought it would be fun to have company. She rented a car and headed north until she came to a town called La Peñita De Jaltemba where her former sailing friend Fred lived. Together they made the journey and thoroughly enjoyed visiting shop after shop of gorgeous Mexican art work. Just before arriving at their destination they stopped by a roadside stand where a man was selling tacos. Fred asked him what kind of tacos they were and he responded that they were *cabra*. Not knowing what the word meant Fred asked if anyone else purchasing tacos could help us. That's when it was discovered that they were goat tacos. As soon as they were out of earshot they both laughed hysterically. Fred kept warning to watch out for hooves. It was a fun trip. Her friend could be a lot of fun to be around; but for some reason their personalities clashed big time and they always ended up getting into a fight about something stupid. It was draining feeling like she needed to defend herself with him about almost everything. She was finally beginning to reach her limits at having others do the not-good-enough game with her. Enough was enough. It's perfectly ok for believers to hang out with non-believers, but not if they are going to put you down for your faith. That's just not healthy.

The top-loading refrigeration system was acting up and not staying as cold as it should so she emptied everything out and tried to figure out what seemed to be the problem. She thought maybe she had fixed the leak and started the engine to see if everything was now working ok. All of a sudden there was an explosion. A compressor hose containing refrigerant blew. Sophia was knocked out cold. Catherine grabbed her and took her outside fanning her frantically with fresh air. Thank God that revived her. She honestly did not know what she would have done without her dearest companion. She later discovered that it wasn't a hose that blew, it was the heat exchanger. She went into town and found someone who would weld this piece of equipment so that it would temporarily last her until she got to the next port of call with a decent size city. She then found a marine shop and bought some refrigerant. Later that evening she put in a patch to have a new heat exchanger shipped to her in Acapulco. She was always amazed to run into boaters who had no refrigeration. They are the real purists. One guy sailing solo didn't even have lifelines on his boat. Sailing is dangerous enough. His desire to be a purist lacked judgment in Catherine's mind and impeded sanity.

One characteristic common with sailors is that of always being antsy to move on to the next place. She said this even knowing that her soul would find rest in God alone as the Psalmist describes in 62:1. With God as her refuge she would always have a safe harbor because she knew that God was with her wherever she went. Maybe her restlessness had to do with the fact that she was still wrestling with God. There have been times in her life when it seemed like she was at rock bottom. She cried her heart out to God so often and he didn't seem to hear. That would make her feel desperately alone. Was he there? Didn't he hear her? Why wouldn't he answer? Yet he got her through every crisis so he must have heard. She often forgot about the victories when in the next struggle. She really needed to keep a list of every saving grace so she could stop fretting so much. Be there Lord… please she cried?

For a few days it rained so she pretty much just stayed below decks and did some chores like scrubbing the floors, re-arranging the hanging closet and drawers, polishing the bookshelves, that sort of thing. She made a squash cake from a recipe that another boater gave her and it was delicious. She also had a recipe for how to make home-made granola and mixed up a batch. Someone else gave her a recipe for some home-made Kahlua-like coffee liqueur and she made some of that too.

Catherine loved the smell of the rain. She loved the sound of the rain. She loved the gray skies that didn't hurt her eyes. One of these days she was going to go north. Her anticipation was building and she was beginning to hate the fact that she was going in the opposite direction of the desire of her heart. The rain finally stopped and she was getting bored out of her skin, so it was time to move on.

Squash Cake

3 well-beaten eggs

2 cups of sugar

1 cup of oil

2 cups of grated and packed Mexican squash (or carrots will do)

2 cups of flour

1/2 teaspoon of baking powder

2 teaspoons of baking soda

1 teaspoon of salt

3 teaspoons of cinnamon

A dash of nutmeg

3 teaspoons of vanilla

1 cup of nuts

1 cup of raisons

(Coconut makes a great substitute for the nuts and/or raisins)

Beat eggs well

Add the other ingredients

Grease and flour pan

Bake approximately one hour at 350 degrees

(Boat ovens can be tricky – need to watch)

Frosting

3-ounce package of cream cheese

1 teaspoon of vanilla

1-1/4 cup powdered sugar

1/2 cube butter

Granola Cereal

1/4 cup of oil

1/3 cup of honey

3 cups of quick oatmeal

½ cup, or more, of nuts, raisins, grated coconut

Cinnamon and Nutmeg to taste

Heat oil and honey over low heat, stirring carefully until warm and blended

Mix oatmeal with other ingredients

Pour honey mixture over and blend well

Place in flat pan

Put in 350 degree oven for 25-30 minutes

Stir twice

Should be a little brown

Kahlua

Boil 1 cup of water

Add 1 cup of sugar and 2 Tablespoons of coffee

Cool

Add 2-1/2 cups of Vodka and 1 teaspoon of vanilla

Meditative Prayer

The only one we have to please in this life is you dear Lord. No boss gives us an evaluation of our performance on earth as children of God. We are our own self evaluator under Holy Spirit's guidance. In partnership with God we are our own rater of the quality of our existence. If we do a poor job, we suffer the consequences. In a job, we must do well for the boss and our colleagues. The company's mission is god. How much better it is in knowing the highest mission is following through in God's perfect mission of love. When we do well loving God and others, then we have the satisfaction of knowing we're making God smile. There is no higher reward that we need seek beyond his approval.

Journal Prompt

Where do you feel trapped in by society's norms? How can you run to Jesus when life is overwhelming?

Chapter 22

FROM ONE TOURIST TRAP
TO THE NEXT

Catherine left the Bay of Banderas and waved good riddance as she passed Yelapa. The wind kicked up and she sailed wing and wing until she reached Ipala where she spent a rolly and unpleasant night. The next morning the wind hadn't picked up yet but she badly wanted to be out of there so left before dawn under power staying fairly close to shore. At first light she saw some locals waving to her to come and help them. They were having trouble getting the outboard started on their *ponga* and asked for a tow. She only needed to tow them a short distance before they were able to get the motor started. They gave her a couple of snapper to show their appreciation. The anchorage at Chamela that night was rugged but very pretty. Catherine felt a bug coming on and spent the next day in the V-berth. There seemed to be an abundance of red tide in patches. She couldn't but wonder if the snapper she ate and the red tide had anything to do with why she wasn't feeling so great. The next day she felt somewhat better. However, spending hours replacing the plumbing fixtures under the sink because the salt water pipe was leaking wasn't exactly her idea of a good time.

The next destination was Tenacatita. It was blissfully calm and she had the anchorage all to herself. The landscape was very rugged and magnificently beautiful. She rowed the dinghy ashore and found a stream that was shimmering with a gorgeous shade of green. The water was so clear that she spent a couple of hours taking turns luxuriating in the cool water and dreaming on the beach under the shade of a tree. The next day she put on her hiking boots and went for a very long hike. The most unnerving part of that hike was coming across several bulls in an open field. She backed away as quickly as she could trying not to make any noise. They didn't seem to care in the least that a human was in their space. Catherine didn't know that bulls could be peaceful. She only knew of them from watching bull fights on television. She sure hoped being in a ring was not their fate. What a cruel and unfair so-called sport. When she got back to the anchorage there were four other boaters intruding on her secluded haven. She's a friendly soul though and ended up exchanging books with a very nice elderly couple. Then they went ashore and treated themselves to some ridiculously expensive piña coladas at one of the beach restaurants. How sad to see that tourism had reached them too. Nevertheless, she enjoyed Tenacatita so much that she stayed there several days just being lazy.

One more stop before heading to Manzanilla. She read that Navidad would be rather rolly. It was, but not as bad as she thought. The worst part was the density of siphonophores. No swimming in this anchorage. However, it was a relief to discover that not all the anchorages along the Mexican mainland had murky water. After only a one-night layover she moved on.

Manzanilla offered two kinds of attraction for Catherine. She anchored just off the famous Camino Real Las Hadas resort (where the movie "10" was filmed) in the middle part of the divided bay tucked in behind Peninsula De Santiago. From there she could take a bus to visit the southern part of the bay which was a very busy sea port crowded with all kinds of ships. Las Hadas is Moorish by design. The dazzling white hotel rooms with the red-tiled roofs lining the hillside were the stuff of picture postcards. Boaters inside the marina could take advantage of swimming in the pool. She was anchored outside of the marina but did manage to sneak onto the grounds anyway pretending like she belonged there. Sometimes being single, blonde, and tan had its advantages (She was not proud of saying that, but it was true). She sat in a chair by the pool and stared in amazement at the iguana sunning itself on the island in the middle of the pool. It probably had access to the pool without paying a dime. You would never see anything like that at an American resort. What a shame. It was fascinating to watch. One of the guys working the pool area brought a friend of his over to spend some time with Catherine. Taco the parrot was friendly enough, and thankfully didn't bite, even though she was told he had quite the reputation for doing precisely that very thing.

The downtown area across the bay from the resort was a true non-touristy Mexican town. Fabulous! There were so many locals shopping and she really enjoyed the adventure of being in a culture not her own. The women all dressed up for the occasion of shopping by wearing very feminine dresses. It was fascinating watching them walk so gracefully and effortlessly in their high-heeled shoes on the jagged cement streets. Catherine knew that she would have broken an ankle for sure. The men were also dressed very classy in their un-tucked pressed white shirts with subtle embroidery running vertically down the front, light-colored dress slacks, and polished shoes. Intermixed with these up-and-coming citizens were the poor who also lined the city streets. She got into a conversation with one of the women. Maria was plucking some feathers out of the chicken that Catherine ended up buying. Bless her heart. She offered to educate her on the safest way to purchase beef. While her daughter watched the stand she took Catherine to the local *carniceria*. She didn't need to understand explicitly what she was saying in Spanish. First she steered Catherine away from the meat that was in the bin attracting flies. Who buys that? Then she was instructed to watch Maria closely as she ordered some freshly-butchered meat. She scolded the person helping us to make sure there wasn't any meat left in the grinder before adding the new purchase. Catherine hadn't eaten meat in a long time. Now she had a chicken and some hamburger meat. As an added bonus she shared with me how to make *albondigas* (Mexican meatball soup). She guessed that she had interpreted Maria's recipe instructions pretty well because she later made the soup and it was delicious. It was a genuine pleasure meeting Maria and spending some time with her. It was so much more satisfying than cocktail hour with party animals. Catherine admired the dignity and pride of the people she'd met in this culture. No matter their status, they all seemed happy. They were gracious and kind.

The shops were painted in bright colors with gaudy signs. One lesson she learned had to do with the seriousness of siesta time. Any shopping had to be timed around siesta. All the hustle and bustle of shopping comes to a complete halt during the heat of midday. Literally nothing was open. How wise of them.

The town then comes alive again much later in the afternoon and stays active until the wee hours of the morning – or so Catherine had heard. She's a morning person herself so she typically missed out on the festivities of the evening. Every Mexican town of any size has a plaza and it is such a delight to stay up at least once in great while and watch all the action happening in the center of town. It appeared as though all the teenage girls were escorted by an older woman who tagged discreetly behind them. But their shadowy presence didn't seem to get in the way of these young women flirting and swaying to the music of the live mariachis. The beautiful young men did their best to discreetly flirt back without upsetting the girl's escorts. Catherine guessed that they somehow found a way to come together.

It came as a complete surprise to her to be so fascinated with all the huge ships in the harbor. There were tankers, freighters, cargo ships, military vessels, and others that she didn't know how to identify. And they were huge, especially when compared to her little sailboat. She was completely in awe watching these enormous ships entering and departing the port. And she absolutely loved being in a real Mexican town that wasn't designed for the American or Canadian tourist. She could easily imagine herself being a ham radio operator aboard some freighter hauling cargoes to exotic ports around the world. For her personally, she knew not why, this fantasy held so much more appeal than traveling to these same destinations aboard a luxury cruise liner. And she knew it was possible to take cruises on freighters.

After a few days she departed at 0300 to arrive at the very rolly Maruatas by 1700. It was a pleasant sail. She enjoyed reading while underway when the wind was steady and the sails were set perfectly to move Whispering Spirit along at a comfortable pace. The prevailing wind tended to be mostly southerly along the Pacific coastline of Mexico. Since she followed the coastline, most of her sailing was done wing and wing. Occasionally she would have to do some tacking when the wind turned northerly, but that didn't happen very often. On a beautiful day when the wind was just right, tacking can be fun even while challenging at the same time. It takes longer to make headway, but when there's no rush, tacking gave her an opportunity to hone her sailing skills. On this leg of her voyage she saw a very large shark, another sea snake, and a large ray.

Lázaro Cárdenas was about 50 miles (or 93 nautical miles) from Maruatas. If the wind stayed steady she could hope to make anchorage before nightfall if she left well before dawn. She seldom minded leaving an anchorage in the dark, but she hated arriving in the dark. She got underway around midnight. Getting the mainsail up when the swells were rolling in felt like being once again on that proverbial hobby horse. It was fun. She started the engine and headed out slowly pointing into the wind. Then she took the straps off the mainsail. Her harness kept her securely attached to the mast while she hoisted the halyard at first by hand and then with the winch handle to cinch it up tight. Heading into the wind kept the mainsail and the boom freely swinging straight back. Then from the cockpit she released the furling line of the jib cleat and pulled the jib line around the winch and cleated it off when the sail was full. After that she shut the engine down (her favorite thing to do) and then trimmed the sails the way she wanted them for the best efficiency. She enjoyed this long run. Sailing helped her to feel alive, free, and untethered from any claims of inadequacy. The moon and the stars provided enough light to silhouette the land. The depth sounder kept her alert to maintaining her distance from any shallower water. The air felt soft and pleasantly cool. She was consciously aware of being peaceful. How is it that she could allow others to say unkind things about her abilities? Rather, how is it that she could *believe* the unkind comments of others. She mentally checked off all her personal achievements. Why do some people feel that they have the right to belittle others? Bullies were her worst enemies. But maybe

God allowed them in her life so that she would be reminded not to intentionally hurt others, not that she would. She believed herself to be kind, at least most of the time anyway. Enough of that kind of thinking! Right then she felt glorious. She tended to be a worrier. Maybe being that way is good at times because it keeps her antennae up to any lurking problems. She determinedly gave herself a break from thinking and just relaxed into the joy of the moment. Imagine a happy Jesus. There are a few pictures of him smiling and they are delightful to behold.

Nearing Lázaro Cárdenas was surreal. First, she was boarded yet again by officials off another Mexican Navy ship while underway. Again they approached her in their *ponga* and the two who came aboard Whispering Spirit were very polite and apologetic, as usual. All they wanted was to see her papers for being in their country. Their visit was very brief. All Catherine's paperwork was in order and met with their satisfaction.

She didn't have a chart of the area and was challenged to find the entrance to this enormous shipping port which was much grander than Manzanillo. It was especially spooky with the diminishing light of day and being confronted by large waves with white caps that seemed to hover at what she initially thought was the entrance. She finally did find the real entrance and anchored just inside the breakwater. Come daylight she saw quite a lot of Russian ships and a Nationalist China freighter.

The next stop was Isla Grande and then Isla Ixtapa. The most interesting sight while sailing was a bird sitting on top of a turtle – at sea. Talk about cultural diversity! Catherine was glad God created such variety. As a teenager she used to volunteer in the nursery at church. She adored those little people who were just learning to walk and talk. The sweetest picture she carries in her mind is the variety of cultures sitting next to one another in their miniature chairs pulled up to a giant miniature table eating their snacks. She remembered twins from India, a precious little African girl who had been adopted, an Asian boy, a curly headed blonde, and a dark-haired boy with the bluest of eyes. It was pure joy to watch them interact without any prejudices. This was role modeling in reverse – the children teaching the adults about what it means to play nicely (well, most of the time anyway). What a sweet depiction of what Heaven will be like.

Lots of tourists visit the island by *ponga*. It was pretty rolly so she headed for Zihuatanejo after a quick lunch stop. The trip only took an hour and forty five minutes. The anchorage was crowded with yachties and the rolling swell followed her in. The next day she explored the town and was surprised to find it to be quite expensive. She visited a couple aboard their boat and learned that they were members of the Seven Seas Cruising Association. She spent the next day topping the fuel and water tanks and stocking up on provisions. She was also fortunate enough to get a patch through to her mom just to say hello and see how she was doing. She felt fortunate having a friend who lived in Rolling Hills Estates in Southern California who was happy to help her make patches on the ham radio.

The trip to Acapulco was uneventful with gentle but consistent winds. She saw many sea snakes and a school of porpoise. Acapulco Bay is very large. The coastline is jam packed with tall resort edifices. Catherine disliked it immediately. The mountainous backdrop was hazy due to some fires that had been burning out of control for several days. After what seemed like a very long time at sea, and with the stress of getting settled in a slip, she was exhausted and spent the next several days just lollygagging onboard. She had to work up the courage, and the desire, to face this gargantuan city.

After regaining her strength, and working up the mental courage she needed, she headed into the big city. She found the Post Office and the refrigeration parts were there waiting for her. After talking with several of the other boaters, she found someone who said he would be happy to help her fix the refrigeration system. That was a huge relief because this mechanical nightmare had been giving her fits and it was nice to turn it over to a willing expert.

The yacht club offered pristine restrooms with hot-water showers. So maybe there was at least one thing good to be said about this place. She took care of the usual city chores and then made preparations to get underway for what she hoped would be quieter ports of call. Walking the busy city streets held just a blur of memories, nothing noteworthy. It was like walking in the big city of downtown Los

Angeles on a hot summer's day, the only difference being that the advertising screaming in your face was predominantly in Spanish.

Catherine's next stops were Bahia Dulce for an overnighter, then Chacahua, another Puerto Escondido, and Guatulco. There was an abundance of wind and she sailed most of the time with just the mainsail. Even with the sloppy seas she managed to catch a skipjack while trolling off the stern. In town at the last anchorage she saw several wild turkeys, hogs, and mules freely roaming the streets. A dead turkey, the kind you find in the grocery store in the meat section, is a *pavo*. A live turkey is a *guajolote*, which is very fun to pronounce and also fun to use for name calling when in the mood to tease someone. I saw a sunken yacht that apparently sank a few short weeks ago according to a couple aboard another boat – very depressing and scary.

Now it was time for some semi-serious distance sailing. Costa Rica was the next planned port of call. The day started out quietly. Then the wind direction changed to the north. As evening approached, the wind veered to the east. It got progressively heavier and the seas came at Whispering Spirit in a short chop. Although Catherine had checked out of Mexico, an emergency prevented her from continuing on. Right off Salina Cruz the engine died. With the weather as nasty as it was, she wanted to go into this port and wait out the storm. But she had to get the engine running first because she felt certain she would not be skilled enough to sail into this harbor. This is about as miserable as it gets. She had to head far enough off shore to be clear of all the many boats coming and going. She furled the jib and let the main swing freely as she headed into the wind before going below decks to see if she could figure out what was wrong with the engine which is located below the floorboard under the steps off the galley. Her stomach was churning with the sloppiness of the seas and a mounting anxiety. It took her about an hour to change the electric fuel pump and get the engine started again so she could power into the very windy port of Salina Cruz, her safe haven for the night.

Catherine wasn't eagerly looking forward to departing for the dreaded crossing of the Gulf of Tehuantepec renowned for its fury of storms. The weather forecast did not indicate any serious weather so she bit the bullet and departed at dawn. The temperature was really hot and the air was dry and she faced a healthy north wind that eventually dropped down to a bare whisper. All in all she was having a relatively peaceful day of sailing. She caught a small Dorado while trolling. Another boat was paralleling her sailing much closer to the shore. It was somehow comforting to have another boat nearby. The next day there wasn't any wind at all so Catherine let George, the iron jenny, do most of the work. The coastline was monotonously flat and un-picturesque, which is why it is notorious for the strong winds that come funneling over the land from the Caribbean side. She decided to make a fuel stop at Puerto Madero and arrived around 1600 hours after two full days and one night crossing the gulf. She felt so blessed to have made the crossing safely.

Precisely at sundown on her first night's crossing of the Gulf she saw *the green flash* for the first time. She had no idea such a thing even existed. She was enjoying a peaceful time in the cockpit watching the sun go down on a clear night with a clear horizon. Just as the sun set below the horizon, there it was, the green flash. It was a sudden burst of beautiful green color left behind by the sun. She was so glad she didn't blink. She looked intentionally for it after that and did see it again many times, so she knew she hadn't imagined it.

Meditative Prayer

Now and then you bless us by flashing your Presence before our eyes. How quickly our thoughts scatter instead of staying focused on such a precious moment. Teach us dear Counselor how to seek you within where we have been taught that you abide. Your sanctuary doesn't always have to be some other place. Help us to quiet our over-active spirit and rest in you. Please make your sanctuary within us so that we can go often and find solace.

Journal Prompt

Have you ever felt like you were flying "wing and wing" where the wind and God's breath were moving you along and life was smooth sailing? Seek the wind at your back and sail away into a heavenly sphere where life isn't fighting you. Go ahead, imagine it for just a moment. Then hold the memory for times of troubled waters.

Chapter 23

WAVE TO GUATEMALA, EL SALVADORE, AND NICARAGUA.

Catherine departed Puerto Madero at the southernmost port of Mexico at 0600 and hoisted the Guatemalan flag. Apparently this wasn't going to be a good day for catching any fish, so she eventually gave up. The next day she powered most of the day. That night there was a dramatic lightning storm making her realize how glad she was to have a lightening protection system installed on Whispering Spirit's masthead to protect the electronic systems onboard. There was no guarantee that the boat would escape damage, but a wise sailor will take any and all precautions to ensure peace of mind. In the morning she saw lots of turtles and a few manta rays that were nearly the same size as Whispering Spirit. The next day proved to be miserable with heavy winds and head-on seas allowing for very little headway. By nightfall the wind had calmed down a bit. However, by midnight the wind picked up creating miserably choppy seas yet again. The next day she felt a deep unease as she was now in plain sight of Nicaragua. The day was also a repeat of nasty weather. This kind of sailing makes for very long days. She spent the time paying attention to the sails, keeping watch for other vessels, reviewing the charts, writing, reading, and cooking simple meals. She couldn't wait to get to Costa Rica.

Meditative Prayer

Lightning and thunder are powerful reminders that you, Dear Lord, are in charge and we are left to wonder at your majesty. Thank you for the staccatos and flashes of your holy presence.

Journal Prompt

Whether the weather is friendly, or whether it is tempestuous, how do you respond?

Chapter 24

NICARAGUA STORY

A big advantage to being a ham radio operator while cruising in foreign countries is having the life-saving ability to hear about local happenings and take any necessary action. Such was the case when Catherine heard traumatic news about a married couple sailing south off the coast of Nicaragua. The Nicaraguan Civil War was just getting started when she was ready to pass by this country caught up in deep political turmoil. When she heard a horror story about a couple whose boat had been approached by a gunboat with armed militants, she was more than a little alarmed at the possibility of the same thing happening to her. Apparently the couple had been sailing too close to the Nicaraguan shoreline. The militants boarded their boat and the couple was taken ashore, separated, and escorted somewhere inland. While they were held captive their boat was ransacked of all valuables before the pirates allowed them to return. She didn't have the full story of what happened to them. Catherine just knew she wanted to sail past Nicaragua as fast and as safely as possible.

She heard a story about another sailor who also got too close to Nicaragua's coastline during this same time of upheaval. Again gunboats set out after the sailboat. But in this story the seas were so rough that the sailboat was able to escape by outracing them. Power boats don't fare as well in really rough weather with angry seas. Catherine stayed far enough off shore and didn't have any trouble. With all her heart she thanked God with genuine praise and a prayer of thanksgiving.

Meditative Prayer

O breath of my breathing, vision of my sight, voice to my listening, caress of my longing, and sweetness to my thirst – naught but you can satisfy. When the tears are spent, and the pain subsides, there you are my beloved, my only love. We want to be with you. Why, oh why, do you have us here? There's more loving for us to do, and receive, isn't there? We feel like a babe crying in the dark. We can't see. But you don't want us to see, do you my Lord? You want us to trust you for our daily bread, our daily sustenance. O what a stern yet patient Father you are, knowing what's best for us while we challenge you daily with our will, not yours. Forgive us.

Journal Prompt

What foreigners have trod upon your space with their greasy shoes? How do you respond to the foreigner who knows not your language of love?

Chapter 25

COSTA RICA

The beauty and serenity of Bahia Elena took Catherine's breath away. She sailed into this circular shaped large bay with no other boats in sight. Ecstatically she stood at the helm and felt a deep sense of awe at the primeval landscape surrounding her. She had just entered an authentic dense jungle and felt a sense of home coming although she couldn't explain why. It was as if her subconscious was returning to an ethereal beginning of time. She sailed very slowly deep into the bay just as the sky was beginning to envelop her in varying shades of twilight. Turning on the engine would have been sacrilege. She had never heard the sounds of a jungle before and wanted to savor every one. She wondered how many eyes were watching her from the denseness of the jungle that belonged to God's other creatures.

All of a sudden colors exploded overhead as a flock of parrots screeched by flying very noisily and seemingly very awkwardly. It was as if they had just been released from a long captivity and weren't yet confident of their flying ability. And then she heard another sound, one that she'd only heard before in zoos. Peeking through the dense jungle were howler monkeys. Their greeting overwhelmed her with a kind of joy like that of a newborn puppy's frenetic tail wagging at his master's homecoming. An indescribable peace draped over Catherine that evening and she savored the moments of discovery by wrapping herself in her favorite blanket while sitting on the boom. The water was tranquil like glass mirroring the stillness in her spirit. She didn't want to sleep. She just wanted to sit outside for hours and soak in the sounds of a primitive and verdant rain forest. Soon a gentle mist began saturating the night air. After securing the foredeck hatch and closing the ports she moved to the covering of the cockpit to continue listening to sounds that eventually included those of a steadily falling rain. The trees soon joined the melody beginning with leaves adding a staccato sound that blended with the symphony being played out all around her. Sleepiness eventually overcame her and she retired to the V-berth to the grand finale of the rain's drumming playing triumphantly on the deck above.

By morning the rain had turned again to mist and then eventually stopped altogether leaving behind just soft gray skies and the faint steady rhythm of dripping leaves. Sometime after she had gone to sleep another couple had claimed Bahia Elena as their harbor as well. They anchored far enough off in respect of our personal boundary space. She recognized them and rowed the dinghy over to say hello. From a conversation they had exchanged over the radio with another boat that had moved on, there was a small restaurant with decent food about a mile down a nearby bulldozed dirt path. It was decided to hike in for breakfast. Birds they couldn't recognize, except for the cacophonous parrots, were busy overhead singing their own unique song. They also saw lots of butterflies that made a clicking sound. How is it that the intricately designed angelic wings of an otherwise creepy bug can elevate it to such a lofty status in our prejudiced eyes? Further on a doe ran across the road giving quite a startle. Next in the menagerie were coatimundies animatedly squealing and teasing each other just like normal brothers and sisters at play. They even followed for a short distance with mom close in arrears. Catherine had never seen these friendly creatures before. They looked just like raccoons, only longer and sleeker. She heard they also make wonderful pets. Costa Rica is truly a tropical paradise. However, paradise does have its downside. A snake also crossed the path. Catherine knew very little about snakes and had no idea if it was poisonous and neither did her companions. She would not likely be hiking any other trails in Costa Rica in the future. For that matter, she may decide not to go for any jungle hikes ever again. At the moment she was feeling quite traumatized by this situation and would have run screaming had it not been for having company.

It was nearing the end of the rainy season. The deluge was falling so hard that she got the brilliant idea of lathering up on the foredeck and letting the rain rinse her off. Wouldn't you know it, the rain slowed to a trickle by the time she was ready for a rinsing. Oh well. Salt water rinse it would have to be. She then got an idea to jury rig a rain catcher by tying a plastic tarp to the lifelines with the rain pouring directly into the water tank. She wondered if there was a way to similarly harness blessings from a heavenly funnel directly into her heart. Actually, she thought God had been doing that all along with her awakened and revived sense of wonder.

After a few days she departed early one morning for Bahia Coco. After the relative solitude of Bahia Elena she was surprised to find this new anchorage crowded with so many sailboats and locals motoring about in their *ponga*s. She guessed it was more normal to prefer companionship to solitude. In a trip to town she met an artist and his wife who had been living in this country for many years. They were sitting at a table next to her at a small café and the man was talking about a painting that he had just finished. Catherine apologized for intruding and shared with them how much she enjoyed artwork and asked if they would show her their work. They graciously invited her to their home so she could see all the paintings he'd completed while living in Costa Rica. His native scenes were quite good, at least from an amateur perspective. This retired couple from Canada seemed quite content to be living in the jungle and didn't even seem to mind the gigantic spiders that were regular visitors in their home. Dean and Ginny became fast friends and enjoyed visiting on Whispering Spirit where they all got pretty good at playing various card games. If they were going to be friends Catherine was more comfortable having them visit her. Their goliath creepy hairy legged house guests were more than she could even remotely begin to feel comfortable around. Then Dean caught her completely by surprise. He asked if he could take photos of Whispering Spirit in order to paint her. Catherine was flabbergasted and honored that he thought Whispering Spirit beautiful enough to want to turn her into a painting. He asked for an address stateside so he could mail the finished painting. What a lovely gift.

After one nasty episode, Catherine made sure any groceries she carried aboard weren't including any of her new friend's species of unwelcome guests. Fortunately, she didn't think any of those dinosaur spiders could swim. But she did unknowingly bring a cockroach aboard once that was hidden in the fruit she'd bought. Sophia was really good about sending out a warning when she saw any bugs on board. She even understands the word. She also knew very well when she was no match for something big enough to look her straight in the eye and dare her to attack first. Catherine knew her sound for warning that there was a bug she was cornering. She made a kind of chittering sound with snarled lips. That was the cue to grab a flip flop to smash the poor bugger. After sniffing the remains of her catch against a bulkhead or the floor boards Sophia felt she had rightly earned all the lavish praise she received. Catherine couldn't even begin to imagine life in the tropics without her trusty friend to save her from cockroaches or other nasty creatures.

The next stop would be Nacas Gola. When not underway, life aboard can seem somewhat monotonous except at times when anchored in a place that captured her heart. After being so enchanted by Bahia Elena she was back to being bored. The pervasive rain probably had something to do with her low spirits. However, the rain did have a positive effect on her wardrobe. With all the fresh water she captured in the dinghy she was able to wash her clothes and have them dry on the lifelines in between showers ridding them of that salty stiffness. With little or no sun for days on end, it did take longer for the clothes to dry, but the wait was worth it. Along the beach she was also able to collect some interesting shells to add to her collection.

In route to Potrero Catherine lost her balance on deck and dropped a whisker pole in the water that she'd been using to try and grab a bucket that she'd accidentally dropped over the side. It took some doing but she was finally able to retrieve both the pole and the bucket. her clumsiness gave her an opportunity to get in some good practice with coming about. From Potrero to Brasilito she had a lovely sail and was surprised to see so many expensive-looking homes along the shore in this town that she'd also seen spelled Braxilito. She dropped anchor and explored the beach where she saw a rather large iguana shading itself under a tree. She knew that a lot of people have iguanas for pets, but this particular iguana looked a bit too large to make a favorable companion. Her next destination was Piedra Blanca. It was a very long sail with inclement weather. Then she was off for yet another sloppy voyage to Ballena located inside Gulfo de Nicoya, another huge inlet. Anchoring in Ballena turned out to be quite exciting because of all the white-faced Capuchin monkeys swinging in the trees. She had heard stories about them being really cantankerous though. Apparently they have a nasty little habit of throwing their feces at you from the tree tops.

Redondo Beach was now so very far away and Catherine was getting more and more homesick. But Southern California wasn't her home any more. The feeling of homesickness was more in keeping with missing being in the United States. She loved learning about other cultures, but she missed living amongst the people of her own culture. And yet, with the world becoming so small, it's becoming harder to identify cultures independent of any locale. And there's beauty in that she had to admit. She enjoyed being around neighbors in Redondo Beach who spoke Spanish and she was doing her best to learn the language. She also respected how Mexican families were so closely bonded. She remembered going to Torrance beach alone and seeing at least a dozen Mexican family members companionably show up to enjoy the sun together. She envied them. Or maybe the culture she missed is that of living on the land instead of on a boat on the ocean. In her reading about the Pacific Northwest she learned that they have a rain forest. Although a rain forest is not a tropical jungle, it has the same lush vegetation. Best of all was reading that there are no poisonous snakes on the Olympic Peninsula.

Catherine felt somewhat ashamed to be feeling such a strong tug on her heart strings to be somewhere other than where she was. She needed to learn to live in the present. How can it be that she is further from where she longed to be yet recognized that God had given her this gift of being in the rain forested sister land of her heart's desire?

She wanted to worship God wherever he placed her and she wanted to find joy in this magical place of jungles and monkeys and flying-free parrots. To be fully alive in the present moment is challenging, but a worthy pursuit.

Four other sailboats were anchored in Ballena with her. They made plans to meet for cocktail hour aboard Whispering Spirit later that afternoon. The conversation was typical. Everyone shared sailing adventures that they'd had so far, talked about what was ahead, and expressed concerns and resolutions discovered about mechanical issues. Like people everywhere they also talked about the weather and the storms of their lives whether falling from the sky or swirling around in our heads and bellies. It was interesting how everyone got real quiet when one of the boaters opened up a conversation about Jesus. Catherine's heart began to beat a little faster, her eyes grew wide, and a smile crept onto her face. Funny how people wear their emotions in the tenseness of their bodies! Some of her companions got real rigid. Some unabashedly displayed disgust. Some got belligerent. Everyone had a couple glasses of wine by this time and honesty found its way spewing out of the mouths of those who might otherwise have kept silent. Catherine found it astonishing that someone who lived and died a couple of thousand years ago could still stir up such emotion. In disgust, all but the couple who brought up the contentious subject began to leave. Catherine begged the couple who had steered the conversation in this polemical direction to linger behind for a little while longer. Her new friends showed no sign of being hurt when the others left. Talking about Jesus was like breathing to them. She had to know more. Some people seemed to believe that Jesus needed to hide inside church walls, as if the God of creation needed to be pigeon-holed inside the walls of a building on Sundays. Catherine was hungry to talk to people about God. When her new friends left a couple of hours later she was sober, satiated, and definitely not bored. She was so glad they had the courage to share their love of Jesus with her. She slept very well that night. When she awoke in the morning they had already departed for their next destination to see who else they might share the gospel with. Mission accomplished. Is that why they're called missionaries?

Whatever God gives us to do at any given time serves some purpose of his that may not make any sense at the moment. The secret is to remain alert and listen for his directives. Prayer requires two-way conversations. The best way for her to actually listen to God was to read the Bible and then think about what she'd just read. So often she could hear God speaking to her in that manner. And he constantly amazed her when he seemed to know daily what verses she needed exactly when she read them.

Catherine loved how God revealed himself to her personally and lovingly through Scripture. She found comfort reading Jeremiah 23:3-4 where God said that "I myself will gather the remnant of my flock out of all the countries where I have driven them and will bring them back to their pasture, where they will be fruitful and increase in number. I will place shepherds over them who will tend them, and they will no longer be afraid or terrified, nor will any be missing." While reading this passage one lonely morning in a foreign country not knowing what the future held for her, she trusted that God was letting her know that he would bring her home again and surround her with shepherds who would help her to grow in faith. She needed to find peace in her situation because she was going to make Costa Rica her home for at least a month. Being underway for long stretches of time got very wearisome. Once again she wanted to settle down. That place was Hacienda Nicoyana.

The anchorage was calm and extraordinarily beautiful with a lovely beach backed by dense jungle. The land owners of the beach off the anchorage obviously catered to the yachties. On shore they had a water pump and everyone was welcome to take as much water as they wanted. Catherine tossed all ten five-gallon water jugs in the dinghy and rowed ashore to take advantage of the owner's generosity. Even sweeter, they provided a shower that had been jury rigged behind some trees that offered some semblance of privacy. Getting a fresh-water shower was always an interesting affair. Because of the mosquitoes swarming the shoreline, she first had to spray bug repellant all over her body before getting in the dinghy. Once ashore she had to turn the water on from a spigot a few feet from the shower head located behind the trees. She made sure that there were no monkeys lurking overhead with evil intent. After showering with her bathing suit on, she had to spray up again with the mosquito repellant feeling sticky but somewhat cleaner than she was before.

Feeling refreshed didn't last very long because then it was time to do the work of filling up the water jugs. There was a hose attached to the spigot so it didn't take long to fill each five-gallon jug. The challenge was loading them in the dinghy so they wouldn't fall overboard while rowing back to Whispering Spirit. Rowing back seemed like it took forever because of the now heavily weighted-down dinghy, and she was actually anchored relatively close to the shore. She tied the dinghy line to a lifeline stanchion near the water tank deck fill cap. She thought her arms were going to break as she used one arm to hold the dinghy close to the boat while using the other arm to muscle the heavy water jugs over the top life line. Had she been smart she would have asked for help from one of the other boaters. Being independently stubborn proved to be a burden at times. And she hated being a bother to others. With all the full water jugs lined on deck, she unscrewed the water cap fill cover and began pouring the water into the tank. In order to top off her nearly empty water tank, she had to repeat this whole process one more time. Last came the part where she had to guestimate how much bleach to pour into the tank so she didn't overdo it. Her poor body had spasms all night from the strenuous exercise. Next time she would ask for help, maybe.

Just when she was feeling her loneliest the most wonderful family befriended her. Three generations lived aboard a 51-foot Trimaran. They ended up spending quite a lot of time together to the point where Catherine was beginning to feel like a member of their family. She was particularly drawn to the children. Anthony had just turned two and his sister Fae was seven. Anthony was a brown-eyed thoughtful blonde wise beyond his young years. Fae had the most strikingly beautiful gray eyes with sun-streaked light brown curly hair. She had an enormous amount of energy and was delightfully cunning in her persuasive zeal. Catherine was mesmerized every time she looked into those magical eyes, as if she could see behind them into the wonders of Fae's inquisitive young mind.

Anthony loved to show off for Catherine. One day she went aboard following a shopping spree that he and his mother had made in town. He had a surprise for Catherine and his parents prefaced his entrance into the cockpit with a dramatic drum roll. Anthony had his very first pair of long pants – with pockets. "Look! I have pockets." He stuck his little hands in those pockets and paraded back and forth exclaiming how he was now a big boy. His crush on her was short lived and Catherine lamented to his parents, with a playful grin, how he had broken her heart. All the boaters gathered ashore at Jesusita for a 4th of July celebration. It was there that Anthony spotted the most adorable little Costa Rican girl about his age and it was all over for Catherine. He left her for a younger woman. Oh how her heart ached.

Anthony's older sister Fae was so dear to Catherine that she started calling her munchkin. She taught all those in her presence a lot about grace. Catherine never felt worthy of the love Fae so freely showered upon her with each visit. Not having children of her own Catherine couldn't even begin to describe how she felt when Fae hugged her ever so tightly every time they greeted each other. She often wanted Catherine to help her decide what outfit her Barbie doll should wear for different play dates. Her father wasn't very happy with her attraction to a doll that, at least in his mind, represented everything shallow in a woman. Catherine wrote her a poem meant to capture his frustration and Fae's fascination.

How can anyone even begin to grasp the fullness of the grace that Jesus bestows upon his children? How can anyone adequately express their gratitude for his atoning death on the cross for sins? Catherine guessed it was all about love. He loved her first and she responded in love by adoring this fully God/Man who she would meet clearly some glorious day. Until then she did see him in her heart. In the meantime she tried to love the people he sent her way. And some like the munchkin make loving so very easy.

The city of Puntarenas was a ferry ride away. It was fun taking the ferry to cross the bay for provisioning and all the other necessary stuff one does when cruising. Even more fun was taking the train

Barbie

❧

Barbie, Barbie, Barbie

All grown up in the hands of a child

What wonders you wield in the imaginings of the mind

One moment a princess, the next a bride

I am her and she is me

We are one in this fantasy

to San Jose, the capital and largest city of Costa Rica. Sophia wasn't very happy with Catherine for leaving her alone for such a long day, but she did fine. Catherine kept the forward hatch and the cabin doors open a notch so Sophia had flow-through ventilation, and her catamaran friends kept an eye on Whispering Spirit.

It rained for a couple of days dislodging a huge tree trunk that came floating through the anchorage. Catherine was the first to see it at a distance and judged that it could cause some damage if it hit one of the boats. Others soon saw it too and a couple of the stronger men got in their dinghies and kept it floating clear of any boats using their whisker poles to guide it along. The heroes were applauded for going above and beyond to protect more than their own skins.

It was time to move on. There wasn't much in the way of wind so Catherine mostly motored to Quepos. A crazy thing happened while she was trolling. A goofy booby bird got entangled in the fishing line. Catherine had a terrible time slowly reeling it toward her so as not to harm her unintended catch. Wearing gloves and a long-sleeved shirt, she did eventually get her feathered friend free.

Quepos was another very rolly anchorage. She should be well used to these by now but acknowledged that most people have stuff that they feel a need to complain about. She wondered how long it was going to take her to be able to walk normally on land again. Maybe that's how the song about a drunken sailor originated. Maybe the poor sailor wasn't drunk at all. Maybe he'd just set foot on land after being at sea. On a trip to town for some provisioning, another snake slithered from its hiding place crossing right in front of Catherine scaring her half to death again. Didn't they know that they weren't allowed on paved roads? More and more she was longing to live where there weren't any snakes to contend with, at least the kind that slither on the ground. Fortunately her faith was becoming more solid. Evil, though still scary, was having less of a stranglehold over her. And she'd read the last chapter of God's love letters so she knew who won the battle, and it wasn't the slithering serpent. Nor was it the two-footed human snakes spewing out their poison on targeted victims.

Still no wind the following day so she did more motoring than she would have liked en route to Cano Island. When Catherine got there she was flabbergasted to see a sailboat anchored nearby from Malmö, Sweden. These *Svenskas* (Swedes) came from the same city where Catherine's grandmother had been born. They sure came from a long way away. She enjoyed cocktail hour with them exchanging stories about the time visiting their home town when Catherine's grandmother had taken her there. Astonishingly, they even knew her grandmother's sister, so she shared a favorite memory with them.

Nanie, her grandmother, took Catherine and her aunt to Sweden when she was nearly twenty. They stayed with her sister, Möster Maja-Lisa (Möster means aunt in Swedish). Her home was decorated with flocked wallpaper; black in the living room and red in the kitchen. She spoke almost no English. On the first night together Catherine remembered that she wore a cotton shift. Her aunt wore a football jersey, sports fan that she had always been; and her grandmother was covered very modestly in a flannel nightgown and robe. Then out pranced Möster Maja in a see-through nightie. Catherine thought her grandmother was going to die on the spot. She yelled at her sister to GO AND PUT SOME CLOTHES ON. Maybe it's true what they say about Swedes being flamboyantly immodest. Catherine enjoyed her visit to Malmö and meeting so many relatives.

Nostalgia crept in triggering another memory. She was sailing in the Channel Islands off Santa Barbara in Southern California and wanted to visit one of the many caves of Santa Cruz Island that friends had told her about. She anchored near the mouth of the cave and rowed the inflatable dinghy inside the large mouth of the cave's entrance. It was bright just inside the entrance, but as she rowed deeper into the cave a flashlight was needed in order to see as it got progressively darker the deeper she went. She wanted to see what mysteries the dark held for her. It was a hot day but chilly inside the cave as the large opening gave way to ever narrowing rock walls the further in she went. When she turned a bend, the sun's light completely disappeared and she turned off her flashlight. Catherine heard a constant dripping sound as sweat dripped down the sides of the cave wall blending with the sea water swooshing against the sides of the dinghy. The tide was coming in and she felt the dinghy gently rising and settling with each new wave. The ocean rises as the moon croons. It's a daily love affair that is never consummated. Sadness overcame Catherine at this unrequited romance and she turned her flashlight back on. At the end of the cave was a rock ledge where seals rested and occasionally barked their forlorn songs echoing throughout the cavernous space. She was experiencing again what felt like the beginning of time, or the end. Her skin tingled with the mixed sensation of fear and awakening. She turned around and headed back to the light of day. Reality can be too harsh sometimes. On her current journey she was entering the end of her own inner darkness. The dawn of awakening was nearing. She could feel it as clearly as she could the tears of time dripping down the hard rock of the ancient cave walls. Solid rock met gentle tears.

Catherine had another memory of sailing the Channel Islands. And this one left no touch of fond memories, only a series of learning curves. While anchored on the lee side of Santa Cruz Island, the wind kicked up and she up anchored and headed around to the other side of the island to see if it might prove to be quieter. It was, but only for a very short time. The weather became so nasty that Catherine felt her only real choice was to head home to Redondo Beach. She was a relatively novice solo sailor at that time and didn't carry any foul weather gear. She regretted this stupidity as the rain pelted her. To add to the discomfort, evening was encroaching fast. Then the engine died in the middle of the shipping channel. White knuckled she clenched the steering wheel as she saw the very large ominous dark shadow of a ship's hull headed toward crossing her path. She had to use all her skills and concentration to hurriedly hoist the mainsail and unfurl the jib so she could sail behind the ship to avoid collision. Finally she was out of the shipping lane. Then the wind all but died. Now Catherine had no engine to propel her and only a whisper of wind to push Whispering Spirit forward in a crawl through the rain. Then the fog crept in. It wasn't long before she noticed the depth sounder showing shallower and shallower soundings. Then she heard the surf. That's when Catherine called the Harbor Patrol. By this time she was near the entrance to the

Portofino marina. To her disgrace she had to be towed back to her slip. She had been awake for 32 hours and completely exhausted. She couldn't wait to get back to the apartment where she was living at the time. After haphazardly getting Whispering Spirit somewhat stowed away, she trudged up to the marina parking lot to drive home. Dear Lord! The car wouldn't start and she had to call the auto club to have the batteries recharged. Catherine was surprised she didn't throw in the towel with sailing after all that.

Meditative Prayer

Candle's light, so tiny, so bright.
I stare at the flame and my eyes hurt.
Lord Jesus – when will you become more than a flickering beacon of wonder?
Fan your flame of mystery. I want to know you more.

Journal Prompt

Do any of your childhood memories have to do with Jesus? Can you go there again in your mind and in your heart?

Chapter 26

PANAMA

Golfito was Catherine's last anchorage in Costa Rica. She spent a couple of days just lounging around before getting herself emotionally prepared to sail to yet one more country. She departed at 0200 for Panama for the long run to Isla Parida. Upon arrival she found the anchorage to be full of shoals and extremely tricky for maneuvering. After an uneasy night, she left early the next morning for a six-hour run to Brincanco. When she arrived there were six shrimpers anchored and she did her usual trading. A very dark-skinned Panamanian came over for a visit. They chatted politely in her broken Spanish while he sat in his *ponga* and talked up to Catherine in the cockpit. She felt very uncomfortable when the conversation ended and he didn't seem to want to leave. She did her best to gesture her apologies that she had to get to work below and he eventually left.

Medidor was Catherine's first visit to an archeological site. It could also be called the site of her gullibility because she believed that the stories about her purchase were true. A local salesman extraordinaire was hawking some artifacts and Catherine listened in fascination as he told her that a statue of a little iguana was found in twelve feet of dirt and was dated around 400 years ago. She paid ten dollars U.S. for her new treasure. She guessed that he had a stash full of iguanas in the shed behind his stand but she really didn't care. They were both happy with the exchange.

What a lovely spot. There were so many *cascadas* (waterfalls). Catherine had often wondered how wonderful it might feel to stand underneath a waterfall. So she did it and it was glorious. The sun was shining brightly on the water and she collected some green river rocks that had the most beautifully marbled strata. Catherine thought she just might treasure the rocks more than she did her collection of shells.

The next stop was Bahia Honda. It reminded her quite a lot of Bahia Elena because it was a large protected inlet body of water. Anchoring anywhere that the water was as calm as glass was a sought-after experience. She was enchanted soon after arriving and getting anchored because all of a sudden from seemingly nowhere a dozen or so *ponga*s came at Whispering Spirit bursting with the shouts of excited children. She had long been prepared for such a visit and gave out pencils and lollipops which naturally turned her into an instant hero. They were all very animated and chatted away in their native tongue so fast that Catherine had a hard time following the conversation. But their body language told her how happy they were to have this foreigner visiting their waters. When Catherine showed them that her party bag had finally been depleted, they were satisfied that they had exhausted her supply and headed back for home. But early the next morning they were back. By this time their cuteness had worn off with so much begging. It was time to leave.

Catherine was really beginning to struggle with her purpose in life. She couldn't come up with one justifiable explanation as to why she was on this journey. She felt a deep-seated urgency inside her to want to give back to society. This trip was too selfish and purposeless. She wondered if people living in monasteries felt the same way. She said that knowing how often she used to think she'd like to live in a monastery. How was she serving God? How was she serving other people? What possible good was coming out of this whole thing? Catherine felt ashamed. God didn't make his children to live in isolation. Catherine knew that she worshipped him, and maybe that was enough. But somehow she felt that it was not enough. She knew we are to love others in addition to loving God. And she believed that was an action word, not simply some internal intangible philosophical spiritual quest. She wanted to be a contributor to society. She wanted to look back on each day and feel like she had accomplished something worthwhile. She wanted to work for a living.

Seeking your face *is* work though, isn't Jesus? But it didn't seem like work. It felt more like she was pampering herself in the most incredibly spoiling way. Jesus filled her with her deepest longings. He satisfied her more than any friendship she had ever known, more than a child's embrace, and more than the exquisite beauty of nature. But she reasoned that she was working. She was working and struggling to find out how she might please God. She wanted to do something that pleased God. But perhaps the work God had for her to do was not physical action. Loving Jesus involves internal work too. Isn't prayer work? Is praying for others a sufficient way to love? Somehow she didn't think it was enough. If Jesus was her role model, then she must act accordingly. But she did realize that loving Jesus as her Lord and Savior meant that she would naturally want to do things for other people. She knew she didn't have to. She wanted to. Doing stuff of any kind wouldn't save her. She knew that. The stuff is just a natural outcome of first accepting that Jesus died on a cross for her sins and that she's forgiven with her repentance.

Her prayer was that all of those months wouldn't go to waste. She was hoping that sharing her love for Jesus in written words would lead others to love him as he wishes to be loved. Please God, she prayed, don't let this trip be wasted on simply moving about from one place to another. She wanted her love to be a reflection of God's love so that others might believe and be saved too. She knew Jesus had forgiven her. How dare she not forgive herself as well?

After eight hours at sea she finally arrived at Naranjo with another rolly anchorage. She had a miserable night and attempted to leave at dawn, but the seas were too rough. Instead, Catherine headed for another anchorage nearby to wait out the weather. Sometimes the charts she had weren't reflective of what was really facing her in an anchorage. She was experiencing this yet again when she saw lots of rocks lurking just under the surface and seemingly everywhere in her intended anchorage. She couldn't imagine how a reef so visible wasn't indicated on the chart. So she tried another spot. There weren't any rocks threatening to put a hole in Whispering Spirit, but the anchorage was rolly, and it was raining, and she was getting very grouchy. She left at first light with the engine dying on her four times within the first half hour. Surely this is what hell is like… misery upon misery. Catherine did finally manage to get the engine going again and got a safe distance from land. Then the wind came up and she was able to sail comfortably all the rest of that day. There sure was a lot of shipping around the canal. She saw so many different country names painted on the transoms of mostly cargo ships. With a full load, some of the cargo aboard those ships looked to be several stories high. She couldn't imagine how they managed to stay upright.

All the anchorages were becoming a blur to her. It was challenging to differentiate one from another anymore. She wondered how she could try to grasp the meaning of so much pain in the world without it becoming just one big blur. The world gets very small when survival on a boat is the predominant discipline of each day. She acknowledged that she was almost an island unto herself sailing around herself. Is our commission to feel compelled to make the world a better place by being involved in other people's business? Maybe some space is needed so people can figure out how to solve some of their own issues where possible. Maybe God wants some one-on-one time with his children so he can be the one to help them. Does God expect people to solve other people's problems while sacrificing their own family unit? And how many well-meaning people keep the other at a comfortable safe distance while presumably attempting to justify their energies of time and money? Catherine knew she was guilty. She knew how satisfied she felt giving money to an organization to sponsor a child on the other side of the world. That was easy. That was clean. And that was good as well. But what if God wanted her to love a child of his who is covered in the filth of self-destruction in her own neighborhood? What if God wanted her to get down and dirty with them right where they are to love them as he loves them? Is that where she drew the line? Is that where she said no and expected someone else to do the dirty work?

If we capitalize the "O" in Other and care for those we are physically close enough to touch, think of how acts of kindness might literally reverberate from one person to another. Is this altruistically too simplistic and naïve? Doesn't kindness generate kindness? Does bullying generate bullying? Pressure is overwhelming to the young who are fighting their way out of confusion about who they are in their society of peers. Some pressures are so formidable that bad behavior carries over into adulthood. Does the blame lie with the individual or with society at large? How can we maintain ethical integrity without sacrificing someone else's freedom? Is freedom always the better choice? Jesus gave us each the freedom to choose. Catherine prayed that she would start making better choices. She prayed that God would give her wisdom to know how to love without imposing and to learn how to receive love while setting appropriate boundaries. She wanted to learn how to be God's hands of kindness and his voice of love to a hurting world. And she wanted Jesus to be her Savior when she was hurting too. She asked God to respond in a timely manner when she cried out to him so that she would know that she wasn't alone. But she also realized that probably showed a lack of faith and knew she still had a long way to go in relating with the God she loved.

She finally arrived at the Archipelago de los Perlas and enjoyed a relatively calm anchorage. She loved exploring beaches. After a long row to the nearest shoreline she was delighted to find a stream that she followed to a lovely lake. So often she experienced the feeling of being in a very primitive place, and this was yet another one of those occasions. However, later that afternoon she was sitting peacefully in the cockpit enjoying a cup of tea when she encountered something so earth rattling, literally, that she was transported from a primeval mind set to a futuristic Sci-Fi thriller in a jarring instant. When it was over she almost thought she had imagined the whole thing. She was anchored in a lovely spot on the west side of an island with a steep hill offering protection from an easterly wind. All of a sudden she heard a deep rumbling and her skin crawled. A fighter jet roared overhead so low it seemed like she could reach up and touch it. And then it was gone. Just like that. Back to the past, or the present, or the future. It wasn't that long ago when the Shah of Iran lived for a short while on one of the Panamanian islands called Isla Contadora. Catherine couldn't help but wonder if the presence of a fighter jet was somehow connected with the political turmoil that ensued when the Shah left Iran.

On the trip to Taboga Island she sailed, then powered, then sailed, and then powered again into the anchorage. She was finally just off the famous Panama Canal. The anchorage was very rolly with a steady rain falling. But the rain was not going to keep her from visiting the island. There were delightfully small winding streets and lots of flowers decorating windowsills everywhere. After her stroll and a return to the boat it was time to head over to the canal itself and get away from such an uncomfortable anchorage.

Meditative Prayer

Do children know if they are poor? Do we? What is poverty anyway? There is impoverishment of the body. And there is impoverishment of the soul. Which leads faster to starvation? Maybe that is why you taught us to pray for our daily bread, our daily sustenance. Without you Jesus, how do we even know we are hungry? Is it the rumbling of our stomach or our questioning tears that somehow satisfies the desire to seek you and find comfort regardless of whether or not we find satiety? You abide within us. Help us to seek you in the other.

Journal Prompt

When you are spent and all your resources are depleted, where is your safe anchorage?

Chapter 27

PANAMA CANAL

Upon arrival at the entrance to the canal Catherine anchored off the Pilot Station. Quite a few of the friends she'd made along the way were anchored there too. Although she had arrived at 1000 hours, the pilot boat captain didn't acknowledge her Q flag until 1700. She had to find things to occupy herself for the seven hours she was confined aboard Whispering Spirit. Only after the paperwork was finally completed was she able to relax and enjoy a peaceful evening visiting with new and old friends and talking through details for making her way through the canal.

At high tide the next day she powered over to the dock and filled the water and fuel tanks. In nervous apprehension mixed with excitement, several of the yachties got together for a meal at the yacht club to further discuss the crossing. The next day she went to the bank and then walked to Pier 18 to get her passport stamped.

With what felt like shame she realized that she was becoming increasingly miserable. She was depressed thinking about continuing onward. Catherine could not see any future for herself sailing that made any sense. And she was terribly lonely. Once so brave about just about everything, she was beginning to feel a desperate fear – of this lifestyle, of having no purpose, of not knowing how to get back to a normal lifestyle, and of not even knowing what normal was anymore. She was in a wasteland and she wasn't even on land. She was so used to having to balance herself while onboard her floating rocking horse that it took a while just to walk normally every time she went ashore.

She wanted to relearn how to walk normally. Her heart goes out to so many of the cruising couples she'd met. Catherine saw behind the bravado of their faces and knew divorce was going to be the inevitable outcome for many of them. She'd heard so many stories about couples throwing in the towel on their dreams. Cruising was not an easy lifestyle.

Worst of all she couldn't feel God's presence. Catherine guessed she was still a child in God's eyes because she wanted to actually feel his presence all the time. It was as if he got off the boat somewhere. She cried out to him so often but he wouldn't answer. She didn't want to doubt his existence. If there is no God then she had absolutely no hope and life would make no sense whatsoever. I know you're busy Lord, Catherine pleaded, but I need you. She was at a loss as to what he wanted her to do. She kept returning to thoughts about why he should care about her. She knew she was a hundred times more fortunate than so many of his children. What right did she have to complain about anything? Her heart went out to the destitute plight of those in poverty walking a death march every day just barely surviving.

The Psalmist wrote, "When I consider your heavens, the work of your fingers, the moon and the stars, which you have set in place, what is man that you are mindful of him…?" (Psalm 8:3-4). Catherine wondered why God should be mindful of her. She wanted to mature in her faith one day soon and know that he was with her all the time without needing signs. Hey, maybe by realizing that signs weren't necessary was a sign of her maturing faith. Maybe she was further along than she thought she was. Is faith contingent upon hope, or is faith simply – faith? When she thought she'd been abandoned, did that mean that she was abandoned? She felt shame. She knew better than to even think those kinds of thoughts. Jesus promises "…surely I am with you always, to the very end of the age" (Matthew 28:20). Maybe Catherine was just allowing herself to dwell temporarily in her own little pity party. Maybe Jesus was guiding her and she was just not being as attentive as she needed to be.

Doesn't God exist even if she doubted his existence? Is God real only if she experienced answers to prayers that were in the affirmative instead of the postponing kinds of responses or, worst of all, having no be his answer? She was thinking like a petulant child. So what if everything seemed to be going wrong in her life? She knew she could trust that there was a loving God who was watching out for her. What if she was living a life that she thought was pleasing to God, and yet her life was still falling apart? What did that mean? How comforting it was for her to know she had a God who had experienced everything that she experienced. How wonderful to know that even Jesus occasionally had doubts. He knew how it felt to feel like he had been forsaken by God and left to suffer alone. Maybe for an instant in time God looked away; but Catherine believed his heart saw everything and cried out to his son the moment his son cried out to him. Their spirit was one. It was impossible for them to be separated. And it's the same with us, his children.

But Thou art God – her only God – and she offered him her life. No matter where he had her she chose to trust him and his plans for her life. She could not live without Jesus. He alone had erased her many, many sins. He alone loved her as no human being had the capability of loving her. He alone is holy and good and the only Son of the living God. This she knew. She just knew. Not from her own knowledge, but she knew this to be true from Holy Spirit. God had her in the watery desert for reasons she could only attempt to understand. She believed. Therefore she was saved. So be it. Amen. His grace is her will to obedience. There is no other way. She believed that Jesus was "…the way and the truth and the life" and that "No one comes to the Father except through [him]" (John 14:6).

Catherine vowed to follow Christ Jesus wherever he sent her – even to the grave. His death was her life. His blood was her cleansing. His resurrection was her eternity. If she was walking humbly with God then she was not seeking Santa Clause or a fairy tale. She was seeking her Heavenly Father with the adoring eyes of a trusting innocent child, his child.

In talking to other boaters, Catherine learned that the custom for transiting the Panama Canal was for sailors to go through initially on another boat. Line handlers are required so everyone can help each other out by transiting with others first. She offered to help

Lorene and Derek aboard their 45-foot sailboat Driftwood. Karen and Howard from Windchaser also volunteered. Mr. Gilbert was the Panamanian advisor. To get back to Whispering Spirit, Catherine took the train and then walked the rest of the way.

One of the requirements of boaters crossing through the Panama Canal is to have the boat admeasured in order to get a navigation permit. Whispering Spirit's Length Overall (LOA) was 32 feet. Her Length at the Waterline (LWL) was 25 feet. She had a 10-foot beam and a 5-foot 2-inch draft. Her displacement was 15,000 pounds and she carried a ballast of 5,000 pounds. With this information, and some other details needed for documentation, she was officially registered and ready for the crossing. Mr. Delgado, the Panamanian advisor, was assigned to Whispering Spirit. He was polite while all business taking his job very seriously, and thankfully so. Although crossing through the canal was an incredibly wondrous experience, it was not a party. The requirement was to have four line handlers, the captain of the vessel (Catherine), and the advisor. Four people off a large yacht offered to assist as line handlers. Another requirement was that the captain was expected to feed everyone during the passage. Catherine hoped everyone would like the meal she had planned.

By 0600 everyone was onboard and ready to go. Fenders were tied to each port and starboard stanchion. Upon entering Gatun Lock Whispering Spirit was partnered with a tug boat. One of the jobs of a line handler is to act like an extension of the fenders to keep Whispering Spirit from any damage. Catherine didn't like the look of crumbling walls in the locks and hoped for the best as they made their way through the complicated procedure. The whole operation was an incredible feat to watch, especially when onboard a boat that's making the journey. The line handlers had their work cut out for them ensuring that the tension on the lines was always taut during the rising and lowering of the water's turbulence while inside the lock.

As an aside to all the action going on in a small boat, it was fascinating to watch the people aboard a cruise ship entering the lock coming from the opposite direction. Catherine could see the faces of

Appetizer

2 cans of refried beans

Choice of chopped chicken, shredded beef, or ground hamburger

3 avocados mashed with lemon juice and salt and pepper

2 cups of sour cream

1/2 cup of mayonnaise

1 package of taco seasoning mix

Chopped green onions

3 chopped tomatoes

2 cans sliced ripe olives

Cheddar cheese

Jicama, or chips, for dipping

Coleslaw

Head of cabbage

Slice in two through the stalk

1/2 medium onion minced

Juice of a lemon

Salt – 3 to 4 shakes, and coarse pepper – 4 shakes

Red wine vinegar – 5 shakes

Accent – 6 shakes

Mayonnaise – 2 heaping serving spoons

Beer Bread

3 cups of self-rising flour

1 can of regular beer

3 tablespoons of sugar

Grease pan and bake at 350 degrees for 1 hour

Mexican Vegetables

6 small zucchinis sliced

1 small onion chopped

1 clove garlic

1 small can of corn

1 small can of green chilies chopped

1/4 teaspoon of oregano

Salt and pepper to taste

1 cup grated cheese

4 tablespoons of oil

Sauté vegetables in oil, cover with cheese and simmer for 20 minutes more over low heat

Fruit Compote

Use any fresh fruit on hand (pineapples, oranges, bananas, grapes, coconut, apples, etc.).

Sauté in generous amount of butter until everything becomes coated.

Add bananas last as they cook fast.

Add cinnamon, a touch of vanilla, a swig of liqueur, and a tablespoon of brown sugar everyone lined up at the railing watching Whispering Spirit. Many of the men seemed to be almost drooling with a desire to exchange places. She could see it in their eyes and sense it by the tension in their bodies. The thought seemed particularly funny looking at them all dressed up in their white slacks and navy sport coats while the passengers onboard Whispering Spirit were dressed in real work clothes of naturally starched sea water cleanliness. Not many women seemed interested in watching the small boats and were decidedly attempting to distract their husbands from the railing. Catherine secretly admired the onlookers and would have gladly exchanged places. Well, not initially, but at that point she probably would have.

The landscape going through Gatun Lake was serenely beautiful. Whispering Spirit had never been on a lake before. This was her virgin voyage tucked in waters with land so close on either side. A strange sensation came over her. Out of the blue it occurred to Catherine that she was peaceful and happy. All these people were on her boat and together they were sharing the work and sharing an experience of a lifetime. It came as a shock to her when she consciously realized that she wasn't alone. The lunch was a hit and she was receiving compliments. The team effort was all so new to her. She found that the tension that she normally carried in her body was simply relaxing into the joy of fellowship. She didn't have to do this all alone. She had friends to help. And although she was the captain, for once she wasn't in charge. The advisor was the boss. What she experienced was profound. No one onboard knew her well enough to see the change in her personality. She was always outwardly friendly and kind with strangers. But inside she was deeply shy and tended to be very private. She had no idea she could actually enjoy the company of others. She needed to explore this new world. Even Sophia was enjoying the company and all the attention she was getting.

Before long they were at the Pedro Miguel Locks where Whispering Spirit triple-side-tied with two other sailboats. This was so much easier because all the boats were relatively the same size. One more lake and then they were in the Miraflores Locks. In the time span of a single day Catherine had crossed from the Pacific Ocean to the Caribbean Sea, about a 50-mile journey.

Her physical crossing of a great land divide was also her spiritual crossover. There was no longer any fear in her heart of going back to her former self. She was a new woman. Jesus had taken her sins and made her pure. God the Father now sees her through his Son. As Jesus is holy, so too now was Catherine. The Father cannot look at her without seeing Jesus first and his work on the cross. She need no longer feel shame for a past that had been erased and forgotten. For Jesus said "Blessed are those whose transgressions are forgiven, whose sins are covered. Blessed is the one whose sin the Lord will never count against them" (Romans 4:7-8). Father and Son were reconciled to their heavenly places following the completion of the work on the cross. The price had been paid. The Lamb offered himself as redemption. When the Father blinked, a new way was made available to enter the sanctuary of grace. She stood in that grace with a humbled heart and contrite spirit. She was forgiven because Jesus was forgiven and because she asked to be forgiven. One of the most beautiful Scripture verses in the Bible is "There is therefore now no condemnation for those who are in Christ Jesus" (Romans 8:1).

Meditative Prayer

Abba, what is trust except faith in your love? We can't say yes to you, and no to whatever circumstance you have us in. You love us unconditionally. By that great love, you are teaching us how to love others unconditionally. Who knows more about pain than you? You watched your son die on a cross in purest obedience to your will. Are we not obliged to mirror your sacrifice when others seemingly intentionally hurt us, and especially when that other person is a person who also believes in your son Jesus? Give us your strength to love when loving is difficult. Give us your eyes to behold the beauty that lies within the soul of the other. Give us your ears to hear what is not being said, what perhaps cannot be said, because we are all frail in varying regards. Give us the release we need in our own frailty to forgive hurts so we can be free and move on. Give us, please, the ability to trust in your great love, so that we can be open to trusting others. Isn't forgiving another a form of trust? How can we trust that we are forgiven if you haven't enabled us to also forgive others? Such patience is too glorious to understand. Let us find rest in the act of patience such as it is until you explain all in eternity.

Journal Prompt

Have you ever been depressed? Are you now? What's the solution? The answer is often within. Pray.

Chapter 28

WOMAN

In a predominantly male-dominated world, Jesus upset the apple cart time and again during his short stay on earth. Jesus clearly revealed that he was the Christ to a Samaritan woman who had many husbands and was currently living with a man who was not her husband. As a Samaritan she was an outcast to Jews. Why would Jesus reveal his identity to a woman? This woman turned out to be the pre-ordained, God-appointed, chosen evangelist for the people of her community. Because Jesus chose her as a witness to him, "Many of the Samaritans from that town believed in him because of the woman's testimony" (John 4:39). The woman told Jesus that she believed that the Messiah was coming and that he would explain all things. Jesus replied "I, the one speaking to you – I am he" (John 4:26).

In another situation a woman was brought before Jesus by self-righteous men wanting to both trick Jesus and condemn a sinner to stoning in accordance with the law of the day. Isn't it interesting that an adulterous woman was accused but not the man also involved in the act? Jesus cannot be outsmarted. He confronted the crowd and asked who of them was without sin. If there was such a man in the crowd, Jesus instructed him to be the first to throw a stone. Even the white-washed Pharisees left the scene. Maybe even they had some sense of decency to acknowledge, even in their own hearts, that they were also sinners. Or maybe whatever Jesus wrote in the sand condemned them as well. There was no one who condemned her and

Jesus told her that he did not condemn her either. But he did instruct her to leave her life of sin. Maybe Jesus wrote in the sand that he loved her and saw her true worth and was telling her not to be afraid. Catherine knew that she repeatedly sinned by being afraid and didn't know why she did that.

Jesus chose another woman to be the first person to see him resurrected following his death on the cross. He did not choose Peter or his beloved disciple John to first witness the fulfillment of his promise. He chose a woman. Jesus told his disciples plainly that he would be killed and then rise on the third day. Catherine personally thought that Jesus' followers simply could not understand. When he died on the cross their hope left them. Why did Jesus choose a woman to see him alive before the others after his death? She was sure he knew that the disciples would doubt her proclamation of seeing him alive. Our Lord consistently elevated the status of women. Did the men begin to understand that they should look upon women in a different manner? Maybe what's more important is that women can look upon themselves in a different manner thanks to Jesus. Who would dare deflate a woman when God raises her status? Sadly, too many men abuse women. But women have the truth of who they are in God's eyes "and the truth will set [us] free" (John 8:32).

Jesus honored another woman's desire to sit at his feet and learn from him. He allowed women to follow him. He set guidelines for the protection of widows. He healed women because of their faith. He disapproved of divorce. He loved his own mother so much that he made sure she had someone to care for her after his death. And these few examples don't even cover all the women of the Old Testament who were true leaders in their day, or the women who came after Jesus.

Catherine met wonderful men who were Christ followers, cherished their wives, treated their employees with respect, and led upstanding lives of high moral character and valor who follow the standards established by Jesus with a heart full of devotion. May God bless these men and create more like them. No one of any gender is perfect, but some seem to naturally rise above the others and Catherine felt so blessed when she was in their circles.

Meditative Prayer

Please Lord; let our stories bear fruit, fruit that will last.

Journal Prompt

Sisters in Christ… Have you ever been cherished for your womanhood?

Chapter 29

GROUNDED

When a sailboat is grounded it is in dire trouble unless it was built for this purpose (like a Trimaran). When a child is grounded it also means something went wrong. Then there is the kind of grounding that Catherine sought daily. To be grounded as a Christian is a grand and wonderful thing. And then there is yet one more type of grounding. Catherine wanted to be grounded on the ground. She wanted to be back on terra firma. She got a slip at the Panama Canal Yacht Club and pondered her next move. She knew where she wanted to live but at the moment had no idea how she would get there. She had been praying a lot for God to show her the way. She was also bursting with the joy of her faith and badly needed to talk to some mature Christians. God answered her prayers one morning while she was having coffee at the yacht club where visitors were welcome.

A group of mostly teenagers with a couple of adults sat down at a table near her and began to pray. Catherine's heart pounded so loud that she thought for sure they would hear its drumming. They were animatedly giving Jesus thanks for allowing them to touch the hearts of some Panamanian youth that they had been ministering to the past week. Catherine didn't think they'd mind if she asked if she could join their table. They warmly welcomed her and wanted to know her story which she gladly shared. She sat stunned as she learned that they were from a little town called Port Angeles on the Olympic Peninsula located in the state of Washington…in the Pacific

Northwest! They were in Panama on a missionary trip through their church. They invited her to join them the next day at the school where they were helping with a building project and she accepted without any hesitation. Some of the children's fathers worked at the yacht club and they had been invited to meet there for breakfast to plan the day's activities.

It's important to be a Christian in community. Only in fellowship did she truly learn. Studying God's Word on her own left empty spaces that she now believed only a family of believers could fill. The potter was putting some added touches to her inner mold.

Catherine's new friends contacted a woman they knew who often rented out rooms in her home to other Christians. Her name is Lucy and she did not have any renters at the moment and said she'd be happy to have Catherine and Sophia come and live with her. Catherine had been contemplating this moment for a long time but didn't have the details figured out. So when the opportunity came along to take her next leap of faith she knew God had approved her decision and the plans came together very smoothly. It was obviously meant to be.

It didn't take Catherine long to find a buyer for her beautiful Whispering Spirit. An older couple was looking to downsize into a more manageable size sailboat for their excursion to Tahiti. She was introduced to their cockatiel named Sneeters, an adorable little bird who was taught to say *Stand Back I'm an Eagle*. God is often portrayed as an eagle. Was this a sign of his approval? Maybe she was being silly, but couldn't God give her signs in any way that pleased him? Whispering Spirit had served her well and Catherine knew she would serve her new owners equally as well. After another week of taking care of the paperwork for the sale and helping her new missionary friends with their building project, Sophia and Catherine and their new friends boarded a plane from Panama City to Seattle, Washington. She was embarking on yet another adventure where she would remain solidly grounded on land and in her faith.

Perhaps the most important lesson she was learning was that being a Christian is a life-long journey of walking with Jesus. Just as the Kingdom God promises are now alive in her heart, they are also not yet full in the sense of eternity in Heaven. And just as she can say that she is now fully and truly a Christian, she did not yet fully understand so many things about God.

There are some Scripture verses that she held especially dear to her heart when her burdens felt too heavy: "Praise be to the Lord, to God our Savior, who daily bears our burdens" (Psalm 68:19); "I removed the burden from their shoulders…" (Psalm 81:6); and "I have made you and I will carry you; I will sustain you and I will rescue you" (Isaiah 46:4).

Catherine was raised a Catholic and had many wonderful memories of the traditions of that religion. She spent a few years as a teenager exploring other cultural beliefs but always went away disillusioned and unfulfilled. Believers are consciously blessed to accept the fact that they have a Savior who knows their pain intimately. God chose to leave his exalted position in Heaven to join in the pain of his children on earth. Lucy spent many a Sunday taking her to different Christian churches in Port Angeles. She thanks God for her companionship and ability to answer the questions she had as she experienced different schools of thought about religion and theology. Lucy went with Catherine visiting denominational and non-denominational churches, and fundamentalist and non-fundamentalist churches. They saw people dressed up in their fancy clothes at one church, and everyone comfortably dressed in jeans lounging on sofas drinking coffee at another. She heard speaking in tongues at one church with a rock band and the words to music blazoned on a screen. Another church used hymnals and followed a very orderly service that had been planned out well in advance. There was beauty in all of them as her eyes were opened to seeing different people worshiping the same Christian God (and there is no other God). The religion of her youth was broadening and deepening and would continue to do so for as long as she lived. Because she had a friend come alongside her in non-judgmental fashion, she was able to see without a plank in her eye that might otherwise have been embedded had she sought God on her own.

Mornings continued to be special to Catherine when she could surround herself with absolute quiet. This was particularly true while living aboard Whispering Spirit. Mornings were her favorite time of day to read God's love letters to her. But she also loved knowing, without having a clear understanding that God was near her all the time. Knowing he's near twenty four hours a day, seven days a week is vitally important. At any moment she could call on him for help. She could communicate with him throughout each day. The veil was rent giving direct access to God, "And when Jesus had cried out again in a loud voice, he gave up his spirit. At that moment the curtain of the temple was torn in two from top to bottom" (Matthew 27:50-51). Communicating with Jesus at any time of day meant she could also offer him praise at any moment. If she was having a nightmare, she felt his protection there too. He woke her up before the dream got too frightening. She wanted to find the right balance between calling God friend and being in awe of his majesty.

One of the things that she found deeply disturbing was waking to later remember the dreams she had in the night. Some of her dreams regurgitated back to her former self. But she had changed and repented of past mistakes. Did she need to re-repent of actions that she had taken in dreams that weren't really reality? Did she control her thoughts in dreams? If she did, then she was sincerely sorry for when those dreams were a far cry for God's best for her. Could she attribute her sinful dreams to Satan's ability to toy with her unconscious mind? What, on earth, do believers do about their dreams?

The hard work of learning how to get close to Jesus was learning discernment. In her prayers Catherine often asked for that ever-elusive wisdom. There were too many books, and many by renowned authors, who promoted a contemplative lifestyle that sounded lovely but may not be Scriptural. That's where she needed to ask for Holy Spirit's help. She needed him to point her to Scripture that either acknowledged what some authors were saying was truth or else put it aside. On her journey of self-isolation she knew it was critical for her to not be led astray. She had to learn to validate what she was reading through the Bible. Holy Spirit guided her to trust him and what's written in the Bible first. Some authors were indeed trustworthy.

Thoughts

Why do they seem to have a life of their own?

Why can't I control them to keep me from harm?

They take on a fabric that's ugly and sewn

With colors I hate that are cold and not warm

They creep in while I'm sleeping in the form of a dream

Is this really my subconscious surfacing in the dark?

I hate this inner me that's ugly and mean

I'm lost in a fog that's built on a lark

Yes, the evil one takes over my mind in the night

Til I awaken in a start all drenched in a sweat

From the nightmares he's stirred up controlling my plight

But foolish is he to take on a bet

With the King of all Kings and the Spirit of Light

There's many a reason I call Him my Savior

From out of sleep's darkness I cry out to Jesus

and banish my fears and Satan to hell

Where he lives in the pit burning with fury

because he knows that he's lost

and he knows that I'm saved

With Holy Spirit she was confident that she could go to Scripture and discern truth.

Like a flame shining through a beautiful candle holder was her spirit now burning within her. She could look back on her life and cherish those moments when her flame ignited a holier kind of passion and her heart's song soared in flight. She wished she could hold on to those flights of ecstasy, but life must be lived.

She remembered her grandfather taking her to church with him – just her – and how special she felt as she sat safely by his side mimicking his motions of worship. She remembered him wearing a tweed suit. He was the classiest of men. He was still alive in her heart and she was trusting that she would see him again.

As a teenager she remembered a time visiting a church on Christmas Eve. The pastor had just completed a heart-warming sermon. The musicians had begun playing some sweet contemporary worship songs. Everyone in the congregation was given candles. One by one each person's candles were lit by the person standing next to them and the flame was passed on to the next person. The room had been darkened. She looked around and all she could see were hundreds of flickering lights throughout the auditorium. She realized later that those were the flames of both that moment and throughout eternity. She was sharing a worship moment with many of her brothers and sisters in Christ. She still remembered tears of joy from having been profoundly touched somewhere deep within her unknowable place that occasionally surfaced and caught her by surprise. Why was there so much dissension in the Body of Christ? Why couldn't everyone be more often like the earliest Christians, where "All the believers were one in heart and mind" (Acts 4:32)? The gospel message is simple. Why do people make it so hard?

Catherine had so many memories that she cherished of her times with Lucy. They went for long walks out on Ediz Hook, the seven-mile spit of land that acts as a safe harbor for boats of all types and sizes. The backdrop of the spit is something Catherine felt incapable of describing with any justice. On a clear day the view is stunningly breathtaking. You first look out across the water, then see the gently forested city, then the sloping hills of green meadows, and then the snow-capped mountains of the Olympics that majestically reach up to heaven. The view was like her faith taking baby steps as she gradually climbed her ladder of comprehension until that glorious day when she would actually see Jesus and the veil would be fully lifted.

One day Lucy and another friend took Catherine on a hike to Marymere Falls near Lake Crescent. A teenage girl and boy holding hands were just beginning their hike up the trail as Catherine and her friends were almost near the end of their hike. The boy tripped over a rock and began screaming in pain as he grabbed his ankle. Lucy was a nurse and asked if she could take a look. He agreed. She volunteered that she and her friends were Christians and asked if it would be ok to pray for him. Catherine was shocked that he agreed. Lucy looked at Catherine and asked her to pray. She was dumbfounded as this kind of thing was totally new to her. In order to not make a scene, she obeyed and started praying as hands were laid on him. After she could think of nothing more to say she stopped praying. The boy had stopped trembling and was very calm. Lucy asked him how his ankle felt and he said that it felt fine. She encouraged him to go see a doctor and have it checked out right away. But he said again that his ankle was fine and the two of them returned to the business of hiking up the trail. Lucy told her after walking away that he was ready to go into shock. Did she just play a role in a healing? From the shock of it she began blubbering uncontrollably. That was a God encounter and she had to acknowledge that what she had just seen was a miracle. And she had to take a moment to bow before God's supremacy. This was not a first for Lucy or her other friend. They were accustomed to seeing God's hand at work.

On another visit to beautiful Lake Crescent she witnessed a most precious and heart-warming sight. Geese were paddling along near the shore. They looked so majestic and regal as if they were messengers in God's court. A mother duck and her brood of ducklings were tucked in along a bank. As the geese swam near her they slowed down and seemed to beckon the mama duck and her ducklings to follow. They waited patiently, like God does. In trust, the little family paddled out to their benefactors who were protecting the little family and surrounded them as they all then headed on their way. Now that Catherine was a professed Christian she too has a new family. She was not alone anymore. She belonged.

Her friend also introduced her to some of the gentlest people she had ever known. To honor her Christian Makah Native American friends she wrote a couple of poems that she hoped would express her deep respect for their culture.

Catherine believed in eternity and life after death, but she couldn't explain it. She believed in faith, but she couldn't explain it either. She believed that Jesus lived (lives) because the history books (Book) tell of his time in a real place and of the lives he touched. She believed he truly died on a cross. There were many witnesses. Real people buried him after his spirit left his body. And real people saw him three days later walking, talking, and eating. Miraculously his spirit returned to him. There were many eye witnesses to his resurrected body. And then he went away again, but not before performing more miracles. He returned to his true form. And he left those left on earth with hope and wonder. She keenly felt his presence just then, although she couldn't explain it. She believed Jesus called her to believe in him. She believed Holy Spirit gave her faith and that he lived within her helping her daily to grow in wisdom. She believed, although she couldn't explain it, that Jesus' death on the cross was an act of substitutionary grace for her repented sins, and that it was a precious gift, and that he was the only way to a life of eternity in heaven. Somehow God the Father saw her now through Jesus. All her sins died with Jesus on that cross forever throughout eternity. With the new covenant the Lord promises that he "will remember [our] sins no more" (Jeremiah 31:34). Jesus is the God of the Old Testament as well as the New Testament. Amazingly, Catherine knew she was clean. Jesus' blood cleansed her inside and out. When the Father looked at her, he looked at her through the loving sacrifice of his Son. She couldn't explain how she knew this was all true, but she knew. Holy Spirit had quickened her spirit and she believed.

Wolf Cry

While walking in the forest all alone one day

I heard the lonely cry of a wolf nearby

He came right up to me and seemed to say

Dear lady, have your plans gone awry?

Or are you exactly where you want to be

On this journey to discover who you really are

We're alike, you and me

As we travel afar

I will howl and you can sing

In harmony we'll praise the Great Eagle Spirit

Until he's swayed to clap his giant wings

In celebration of our wit

Outsider

Being drawn to the Pacific Northwest

was an inexplicable pull that I'm still working out.

Love of forests with horizons of green

pull my heart strings in a myriad of ways.

The healing rains and penetrating sunshine

soak deeply into my depths

and warm the surfaces of residual pain.

The occasional snow is a burst of surprise

in surrender to the majesty of God

and his pure white light blanketing troubles into quiet submission.

Can an outsider claim a piece of this land so rich in the history of First Peoples?

I am but a guest in their land and live in the far, far reaches of their truth.

They are beautiful to me.

My heart beats in synchronicity with the rhythm of their drums.

I should have been born an Indian.

I think I understand, though I probably don't,

their gentleness and fierceness in harmony with nature.

But I *am* a woman after all

so how far outside can I possibly be?

It was so very painful to think that not everyone gets saved for spending an eternity with Jesus in his kingdom yet to come. Catherine didn't know how to reconcile that with people she loved who scorned Jesus. She could live with this heartache if she thought that people just simply die and lay fallow as ash, but that's not what God's Word teaches. This was her heartbreak. She prayed that her story would make a difference in the lives of those who won't believe. She prayed that her story would help women to fully realize how much they are cherished by God. And she prayed that her story would open up ways that she couldn't even imagine for others to have a deeper relationship with Jesus as they see their own story in some of what she was sharing.

God loves her so much that he's finally giving her the courage to trust him, and him alone. She used to think that just about everyone else was smarter than she was. She used to think that leaders, and especially leaders with power, were so much wiser than her. But Jesus says "Truly I tell you, unless you change and become like little children, you will never enter the kingdom of heaven" (Matthew 18:2-4). Jesus honors and elevates women and children. Catherine looked back on her accomplishments and knew that she did not need to feel like she had less to offer than anyone else. Why she experienced being bullied by so many people was a mystery to her. Yet all of her successes in life meant nothing when compared with salvation. Jesus' love covers over every achievement list. Nothing is more important than his love. Because of him she could hold her head high with dignity. She saw so many impoverished women in her travels. Yet many also seemed to have an inner joy to sustain them. Her guess was that they knew Jesus.

Catherine longed for her dear sisters in Christ to not be discouraged when life was difficult. She wanted them to never, ever give up on Jesus because he would never give up on them. He IS alive and he DOES love mightily. Believe that Jesus loves deeply and with intervention. Catherine wrote this exhortation as much for her sisters in Christ as for herself. And her prayers went out to her dear brothers in Christ as well. One thing she's learned. She never will be good enough, but she is sinner enough for Jesus to die for her sins so that the Father sees her as good enough to spend eternity in his grace that's beyond comprehension.

Catherine once lived in guilt, self-judgment, and under a cloud of condemnation. Now, when she saw the Shekinah glory of God, all that guilt vanished. The pleasurable task was to allow Christ's very real presence to linger. She used to think that Moses wore a veil after being with God because his face was shining too brightly and would blind anyone who looked at him. But the veil was worn to hide God's fading glory. How can believers be so weak? Even true believers behold majesty and shine like the sun until there's a distraction and the glow is lost. When eternity begins the sheen won't fade because the Son of God will be eternally and visibly with his people.

Catherine knew she was growing in spiritual maturity. Daily he lifted her veil and let her see him more clearly. He was purifying her in the fires of her anguish and confusion. She was learning to keep the words of her mouth pure. When she slipped, she was given a time out to reflect on the pain she may have caused another. Then she was prodded to rectify her wrong, first with confession as he listened to her sorrow, and then with action when appropriate.

How Catherine wished she could attend seminary. She thought it would be pure bliss to study God's Scriptures in the company of other followers of Jesus. Words like righteousness and justification would be made amply clear. Righteousness as she understood it, and simply described, referred to being right with God. She liked how the term was used in the Psalms "For the Lord watches over the way of the righteous...." (Psalm 1:6). The NIV notes for this passage proclaim that God's people present themselves "as those who honor God and order their lives in all things according to his will, in every human relationship they faithfully fulfill the obligations that the relationship entails, remembering that power and authority (of whatever sort: domestic, social, political, economic, religious, intellectual) are to be used to bless, not to exploit."

Catherine's understanding of the word justification meant that believers have been made justified by the blood of Jesus just as if they had never sinned. Imagine! In the NIV notes for Philippians 3:13, Paul helps readers to understand what this means more clearly.

LORD

Lord stay in my life

Surround me

Lord fill me with peace

Your joy's in my heart

I'm filled with a wonder

Beyond all compare

Go with me

Be with me

This day

Sinners do not lose the memory of their sinful past. They leave it behind as done with and settled. Songs rang through her head that brought joy and helped remind her of his incomparable gift.

Catherine wanted to be baptized. She was ready. She wanted to be cleansed in healing waters and become a new creation. Jesus removed his death wrapping. Her larval stage was transforming and preparing to emerge. Keenly aware of her chrysalis embrace, she pensively waited. The most beautiful and dreadful red enveloped her. It was like a blending of the sun's rays of morning and the hues of an intense sunset bleeding through her skin. She was finally free to stop grasping for shards of any residual shame that had lost its stranglehold. The cocoon of her former ignorance was too tight. It no longer fit. She had outgrown its confinements and was ready to fly as if she were the birds who had been her messengers. It was time for her to be a messenger for others.

God spoke and creation reverberated throughout his Kingdom in harmonic perfection. God's tongue was the original voice. Now as she waited for God's return, Catherine strained to hear his voice. From memories instilled in her spirit long before she was born, she knew his voice. He called her and will call her again, and again. Her wick burned bright the flame of her waiting in the impenetrable dark. He's coming again. The oil of her hope filled her vessel in readiness. "For the Lord himself will come down from heaven, with a loud command, with the voice of the archangel and with the trumpet call of God, and the dead in Christ will rise first. After that, we who are still alive and are left will be caught up together with them in the clouds to meet the Lord in the air. And so we will be with the Lord forever" (1 Thessalonians 4:16-17).

Accepting that Jesus was the Christ is the one decision that no one can make for her. It was between her and God alone.

Lord, You Know I Love You

What matter the words, I love you the same

Agape, Phileo, eternally bound

In spirit and truth my offer unfeigned

Thou knowest my heartbeat's sound

In thundering measure I offer regret

How deeply I've hurt you dear friend, my lord

So bitter these tears I often have wept

With sins now forgiven I lift up your sword

To care for your lambs and feed your sheep

I truly love Thee my savior and God

No longer in shame these tears do I weep

By sea or by land in fishing I trod

Now clothed in armor of heavenly might

I'll follow you Jesus into the night

Meditative Prayer

Holy Spirit: you are our chrysalis embrace where we wait, expectant, embraced, rocked, loved, receiving, releasing, passive, silent, and strangely alive.

Journal Prompt

How do you get to being grounded in Christ? Is he your anchor? Are you tethered to him? Stand in awe. Be still.

Conclusion

Imagine GOD knowing that the only way to restore fellowship with himself is for he, himself, to die, thereby putting death itself to death. GOD died a ghastly, humbling, humiliating death in human skin intentionally laying down his life to conquer sin once and for all. Then, by his own intentionality, arose from the grave to give eternal life for all those who believe in his gift and acknowledge Jesus' sacrifice in atonement of their sins. GOD came down as a baby, a boy, a man in full humanity, and at the same time, fully GOD. And all he asks is that sorrow is acknowledged for hurts caused and that faith reins as a guiding light toward eternity. He paid the ultimate price for sin – because he is love. There is no greater love than what he's done. It is the greatest love anyone will ever know.

Meditative Prayer

Let it be as you decree

My will only in accordance with Thine

Holy prayers in one accord

Incense fragrant, my heart to yours

Hope catches a ride on Holy Spirit's wings

And my soul rests in peace in the arms of my Beloved.

Journal Prompt

Amen. So be it. Thy will precious Lord.

Acknowledgements

I am indebted to family, friends, professors, and pastors who nurtured me toward the cross and acted as amazing encouragers during my faith journey. A special thanks to Forrest.

About the Author

Bonnie-Jean Heather was born in Long Island, New York, raised in Los Angeles, California, and now calls the Pacific Northwest home. Her sailing experiences included trips to Santa Catalina Island, Santa Barbara Island, and the Channel Islands of southern California; both the American and British Virgin Islands; the Sea of Cortez; the pacific coastlines of Mexico, Guatemala, El Salvador, Nicaragua, Costa Rica, and Panama; and the San Juan Islands of Washington State. She has her Professional in Human Resources Certification, is a Society for Human Resource Association Certified Professional, received a Certificate in Christian Foundations from KOINOS, and has a Bachelor of Arts degree in Business Management and a Master of Arts degree in International Care & Community Development both from Northwest University in Kirkland, Washington. She is a Board Secretary for the Pacific Association for Theological Studies. Bonnie is a passionate disciple of Jesus.

This work includes an award-winning poem, *A Protestant's Adoration*, from the Writer's Digest 80th Annual Writing Competition.

Printed in the USA
CPSIA information can be obtained
at www.ICGtesting.com
LVHW090601110923
757081LV00002B/114

9 780996 343701